HALLELUJAH

By

Dr. Joseph Micah Ragland, J.D., LL.M., LL.D., Esquire

**Personal Injury Trial Lawyer, Legal Counselor, Joyful Good News
End of the Age Speaker, and World Evangelist-Ordained Minister.
Former Law Professor, Mississippi College School of Law, and
Member of the American, Mississippi, and Tennessee Bar Associations.
Email: *joeragland@raglandministries.org***

PRESENTED IN THREE VOLUMES
VOLUME 2

Library of Congress Control Number: 2018906207
ISBN: 978-1-878957-91-7
'Let Justice Roll!'
(Amos 5:24)

**Affectionately and earnestly
Dedicated to the**

**The Father,
The Son,
The Holy Spirit,**
(Matthew 28:19)

**Those who are invited, and choosing to attend
of their own 'free will,' the Marriage
Supper of the Lamb, Jesus, the Son of God.**
(Revelation 19:7)

✝FOREWORD✝

Eternity! No other message, other than the Bible, will prepare you for **Eternity** better than *Hallelujah* you are holding in your hand! **Hallelujah** is not a fictional work, as it reveals actual legal secrets, is full of reliable evidence, is backed with Scripture, and has the most joyful ending to which the Adventurer is invited to participate.

Hallelujah is a celestial and earthly adventure across time, space, and the invisible, having no previous examples, revealing secrets of what is happening simultaneously in Heaven, Hell, and on the Earth. *Hallelujah* will help you avoid the coming wrath (Revelation 20:15) of God and assist in making you God's masterpiece, one of a kind, now and in the coming ages.

Hallelujah means, '*Praise ye the Lord*' and is one of the most powerful words God has ever given to man and woman. It is the ONE universal word in all languages, said the same with no change of accent. The person who overcomes "by the blood of the Lamb (Jesus) and by the word of their testimony" (Revelation 12:11) finds it easy and joyful to say and sing *Hallelujah*. Acquaint yourself now with the Heavenly word *Hallelujah*, and let the joy, the light, the glory, the praise, and the splendidness of this Heavenly word enter your entire being, It is the one word the saved will take from Earth to Heaven! Teach the word *Hallelujah* to your children and your children's children, and you will have done great work on the Earth. Joyfully join the saved in Hallelujahs, Thanksgivings, praise, and worship on the Earth, later in Heaven, and on the New Earth (Revelation 21:1) for God's saving love.

The Adventurer will use the powerful word **Hallelujah** more-and-more as he or she meditates on the Heavenly truth and humor given to Law Professor, Dr. Joe M. Ragland, God's Ambassador, a man of bold courage after God's own heart, faithful and true, in the anointed message he recorded from Heaven for the people of the Earth in *Hallelujah*. *Let The Hallelujahs Roll!*

"*I* (**Apostle John in a vision**) *saw a New Heaven and a New Earth, for the First Heaven and the First Earth had passed away, and there was no longer any (roaring) sea (only still waters representing peace and security). . . . Now the dwelling of God is with people (saints), and He will live (on the New Earth) with them. They will be His people, and God Himself will be with them and be their God. He will wipe away every tear from their eyes. There will be no more death or mourning (sadness) or crying (no stress or worry) or pain, for the old order of things has fled (passed) away. He (Jesus) who was seated on the throne said, 'Look! I am making everything new*! (John) **write** this (to prepare all people, who will repent, receive Jesus as Savior, and confess Jesus as their Lord), because **these words are true and to be trusted** (for in God you are to trust to the utmost)!" (Revelation 21:1-5) [Emphasis added.]

'*The Lord gave the word (message of salvation):*
Great was the company of those who published it.'(Psalm 68:11)
'*Each man or woman has his or her gift from God!*
One has this gift, another has another gift.' (1 Corinthians 7:7)
'*The wise person wins* (rescues from Hell)
souls (for the Kingdom of Heaven).' (Proverbs 7:30)

The Great Commission
By
Jesus, the Son of God

"*All power (authority) is given unto Me (Jesus) in Heaven and on Earth.*
Therefore, go (Kingly command) and make followers (whosoever of their own free will
repents and receives Jesus as Savior will be saved, as God loves all and does not predestine or foreordain any-
one under the New Covenant to be lost in Hell) of all people in the world (nations), baptizing (immersing
showing they died in the watery grave to the old and raised up out of the water grave forgiven in the new birth)
them in the name of the Father and of the Son and of the Holy Spirit, and teaching them to obey everything I
(Divine King Jesus) have taught (commanded) you. And surely I am (Divine Presence) with you always,
even until the end of this (Earth) age."
(Jesus, Matthew 28:18-20)

"I (Jesus, Son of God) am the way and the truth and the life.
No one (no exceptions) comes to the Father (God for salvation) except through Me."
(Jesus, John 14:6)

†TABLE OF CONTENTS†

VOLUME 2

SEPARATE VOLUME 3 TABLE OF CONTENTS

SEPARATE VOLUME 1 TABLE OF CONTENTS

The **First Volume** of **Hallelujah** reveals that Attorney Job had a law practice on the Island of Atlantis, as recorded in Book Six, Chapters 3-5, and recorded in the unabridged Book 7, Volume One, Chapter 1, of **Love & War**. Angels escorted attorney Job, without Job tasting death, to Paradise before the destruction, by an act of war, of Atlantis. Volume Two of **Hallelujah** reveals that Job returned to the surface of the Earth as a baby and again practiced law (Job 9:2, 29:16, 21, 38:33), and *'was the greatest (included being the riches) among all the people of the East.'* (Job 1:2)

Volume 2 of **Hallelujah** further reveals how Attorney Job legally finalizes the land deeds to the Promised Land of Israel, placing them in sealed Clay Jars on Noah's Ark, later to be given to Abram (Abraham), as God legally gives this land to Abraham. Jurisprudentially, the legal career of Job should be studied in *Hallelujah* by both judges, lawyers, and law students, especially Job's ethical violation, his defense of untrue charges made against his integrity, and his legal skill and wealth in obtaining the deeds to the promised land for God to give the promised land to Abraham and his descendants.

✝PERFORMANCE NOTES AND INQUIRIES✝

The author inserts `Courier Font Type` as joyful guidance for the performers, singers, adventurers, and producers for stage performances of the selected scenes. Permission to perform any part of this production in public must first be obtained in writing from the copyright holder Joe M. Ragland. Your requests can be sent by email to joeragland@raglandministries.org, subject line *Hallelujah*, giving a contact name, address, and a telephone number to review the proposed starting and ending dates and plans for the performances, and to discuss the notices, programs, answer questions, need for consultations, et cetera. Freely these Heavenly messages and truths were received and recorded for the people of the world by Dr. Joe M. Ragland, and with quality assurances, permission should be given and maintained for the performing rights. *'Freely these (truths with supporting Scriptures) were received, and freely they will be given'* (Matthew 10:8) to help the teachable people of the world *'to know the truth, and the truth will set them free!'* (John 8:32) Written permission and a reasonable licensing fee must be paid or waved whether a play or movie is performed for non-profit or profit, and whether or not admission is charged. Enhanced script words for the scenes to be performed can be further provided by the copyright holder, Joe M. Ragland, *via* email to be given to individual performers.

✝A New Birth Prayer adapted from the unabridged Love & War, amazon.com, Books by Joe Ragland✝

Please consider praying, even if you are born again, as you proceed 'line upon line, line upon line, a little here, a little there' (Isaiah 28:10) with truth building upon truth in your adventure of adventures in **Hallelujah**. If you get bogged down like regarding the wilds of Job's first wife, who advised her husband Job to curse God and die (Job 2:9), please do not stop, but skim over to the next truth and proceed running your race to the grand conclusion on the New Earth to which you Adventurer is invited to be a part.

"Dear Father God in Heaven, Thank You for loving those in the world so much that you gave Your one and only Son, Jesus, that whosoever (that's me) *believes in Him shall not perish* (in Hell) *but have eternal life. (John 3:16) I know I am a sinner. I am sorry for and repent of my sins. I do believe Jesus is Your Son and that You sent Him into the world to die on a cross to pay the penalty I owe for my sins. Father, I believe You raised Jesus from the dead. Now of my own free will, I receive Jesus as my Savior and confess Jesus as my Lord! I ask the Holy Spirit to come into my heart and join with my human spirit and make me born again. I will not be ashamed to confess the name of Jesus to others! Father, please give me wisdom and understanding now as I proceed through the Message in Love & War, supported with Scripture, to the people of the world recorded by Dr. Joe M. Ragland. I offer Hallelujahs, Thanksgivings, Praise, and Worship for Your saving love for me. In Your Son Jesus' name, Amen* (So be it!)*!"*✝

✝OUR JOYFUL PATH TOGETHER TO THE CELESTIAL CITY✝

You are invited to receive End-Time emails (we will not share your email with others) updates from the Author of **Hallelujah,** Dr. Joe M. Ragland, a friend of Jesus, rejoicing that his name is written in the **Lamb's Book of Life**. (Luke 20:10) As you communicate with joeragland@raglandministries.org, please start with *Hallelujah,* introduce yourself, what has ministered to you, include your first and last name, your talents and gift(s), and your location on the Earth. God has lost people He loves throughout the world to reach. Every life that is touched is a life we reach together. Let us join in Hallelujahs, Worship, and Praise now and throughout eternity for such a joyful salvation as we bring glory to the Lord Jesus Christ! Rest assured your communication shall be appreciated very much! Bless you!

ADAPTED FROM THE UNABRIDGED
www.amazon.com Books Love & War by Joe Ragland
LOVE & WAR, JOE RAGLAND, AMAZON.COM BOOKS
www.raglandministries.org/loveandwarbook/
BOOK NINE – Chapter 1

Scene Forty-Two

Attorney Job Returns as a Baby to Second Earth Age

HOLY SPIRIT DESCRIBES

Uz who had married one of Enoch's daughter's, Edom, whose brother was Methuselah, (Genesis 5:27) chose the lush plain of the Jordan River just North of the Dead Sea to stake out a large parcel of land, known as the Land of Uz. (Job 1:1) Uz consecrated the land to the Lord for the planting of crops, grazing of cattle, the raising of a family, and the worship of God.

Uz and his wife Edom initially could not have children. Uz and Edom obtained four children from orphanages and brought them into their loving homes to raise them in the ways of the Lord.

After the children had grown, they each moved to the nearby City of Zion, the two daughters marrying bankers, and the two sons opening a prosperous lumbering business.

UZ: Uz one day said to his wife, "I know how much you would have liked to have had a son of our own. I told God if He would give us a son I would dedicate him to the Lord. A man of God walked by while I was out in the field meditating on the goodness of God and decreed smiling, '*By this time next year you will have a son.*'(See like words to Abraham in Genesis 18:10) I'm in the mood for romance in the hay are you?"

EDOM: His wife replied with a smile, "It is the proper time of the month. I love you so much. You are a good lover, kisser, husband, and soon to be a papa. It would be such an honor to give you a son. I dedicate our son to the Lord before he is conceived, which could be momentary from that look in your eye. Let me grab the purple blanket and bouncy romantic pillars as we have soft new straw in the barn loft as we watch the beautiful sunset and enjoy the gift of romance our loving Heavenly Father has given us as husband and wife."

THE HOLY SPIRIT DESCRIBES

Uz opens the upper loft windows of the barn fastening them back as the sun and the clouds give off brilliant colors as if to say, "*Let me help you celebrate the romance (mating) time.*"

Edom glowing with joy spreads the blanket, places a large pillow for their heads, and sprinkles exotic and romantic spices over their marriage bed. Uz remarking, "You are altogether lovely to me. I have never seen such a beautiful sunset. It will set in seven minutes. Let us first watch it set beneath the horizon. God's ways and timing are perfect." Edom romancing,'*Make haste, my lover, come quickly like a gazelle, leap for joy like a wild stage on the spice mountain.*' (Song of Solomon 8:14) Uz replied, "Wow, my love! I give God all the glory for giving me such a beautiful and warm virgin wife. Thank God, for a thing called Romantic *Eros* Marital Love! There will never be found anything as strong as love! Wow!" Nine months later from the 'Wow Day,' Edom delivers with virtually no pain a son and suggests they call him "Happy." Uz said, "No my love. The Lord has already named him, Job. Somehow he must have been called Job in a previous life. Job, was a happy child as he '*grew in wisdom and stature, and in favor with God and man.*'(See these words spoken about Jesus, the Son of God, born flesh, blood, and bone in the Third Earth Age found in Luke 2:52.)

When Job was twelve years old, he had a recurring dream in which he found himself also as a twelve-year-old in a delightful tropical paradise. In his dream, he would see himself climbing to the top of a great dividing wall praying that his Creator, God, would bless his day as he sat down on what he called "Meditation Rock" to admire God's sunrise. The lad Job carried with him a backpack filled with carrots, apples, pears, and vegetables to treat his pets in both Dinosaur Country and the lagoon. In Job's dream, his pet was a Bronco, being a baby dinosaur whose neck lifting his head up to the top of the wall to receive treats. Bronco enjoyed so much Job patting him on the head and rubbing him under his chin with Job asking him such questions as, "Do you have my backside covered?" Bronco would wag his long tail affirmatively flattening the thick jungle. Job had also treated Bronco's friends Stego, Tyran, Diplo, and Behe. As Job climbed down his young pet in the sea, Levia would meet him and breathe out fire with Job throwing down various fruit for Levia to catch in his mouth. Job would also ask Levia, "Do you have a defense for God's friends and me if we are ever attacked?" Levi shooting fire out of his mouth like a flame thrower seemed to answer affirmatively. Job once asked his dad in the Second Earth Age after such a dream, "Why did God create long neck dinosaurs?"

UZ: Uz, after acknowledging the Lord for wisdom, answers, "Well Job I understand back in the First Earth Age, before the ice came so suddenly upon the Earth as shown by some dinosaurs being found frozen in glaciers with the green plants they were eating still in their mouth, this Earth was full of dense and gigantic plant life. Perhaps the long neck dinosaurs kept certain types of lush plant life under control and cleared paths through the jungles. Dinosaurs using their long necks could eat the high leaves from the tops of tall gigantic trees. In a thick forest, this would let sunlight come down to the ground so smaller plants would grow thick to fulfill God's purpose for their lives also."

JOB: Job inquired further, "What purpose could God have for all these little plants growing beneath the trees."

Uz, looking down into his human spirit asked for wisdom from God, and replied, "The Holy Spirit says, 'Black Gold – oil!' Job this black gold must be for some purpose of God to benefit humanity in the future. All that chomping by the dinosaurs had a purpose!" (Laughter)

When Job was fourteen, he had another dream. In that dream, Job was on a paradise island wearing a white dressed shirt with a red bow tie with gold scales of justice on it.

In the dream, Job was coming down from his special meditation place carrying his empty bag after treating his pets Bronco, who had fully grown into a 70-foot long, weighing 30-tons, dinosaur, and Levia, who had grown into a 'large sea monster' capable of throwing flames of fire for fifty yards.

Job as was his custom asked each of his pets, 'Do you have my backside covered? And do you have a defense of God's friends and me if we are ever attacked from the sea or by land?' Both wagged their massive tails affirmatively. Job then looked over and saw a sign saying, 'Job – Attorney & Counselor at Law.'

In this dream, Job was highly respected in the community and '*knowing he had influence in court.*' (Job 31:21) Job woke from his dream being so full of joy knowing he had helped so many people with legal matters. Job knew that he had been given a unique gifting and insight into right and wrong, legal and illegal, advisable and inadvisable.

Job's legal counsel in the First Earth Age was greatly sought, and he was held in such high esteem and respect. In the Second Earth Age, like in the First Earth Age, the only way to become a lawyer to enable one to legally advise, guide, and counsel and even be an advocate in court for those seeking to live peaceably with their neighbor according to the law of the land, would be to study law under another lawyer for seven intense years.

Uz's personal lawyer was a William Whitestone in the nearby Land of Zion. Job always begged his dad to travel to the Whitestone Law Office to listen to and observed his dad receiving legal counsel and wisdom from Whitestone. One of Whitestone's favorite sayings was '*Acknowledge the Lord in all your ways,*' (Proverbs 3:6) and '*Let justice roll!*' (Amos 5:24) Whitestone took a liking to Job as he had no children, and allowed Job to stay in the law office and use his private back spare room to study and take a nap on a bed while his dad conducted other business in the city.

WHITESTONE: One day when Job was only sixteen, Whitestone propositioned Uz, "Your son has favor with God and man! He could give Godly legal counsel to many and would have such influence in Court if he became a lawyer. He has a real love for right and justice!

258

I need some help around the law firm. I have this back room, I could spruce up for him to serve both as an apartment and study. He could read law under me, carry my law books to the Courts, help me organize my cases, and deliver legal documents.

Like you, I am very wealthy, and you would not have to pay me anything, as your son will earn his keep. Many wonderful clients like you have blessed me. Job needs legal training to carry on for me after you and I go on to our eternal reward. He will be free to see you as often as you desire. Please don't give me a decision today, but talk it over with your son and if the answer is yes, just bring some of his belongings and prepare to leave him here on your visit next week to sign your 'Will' leaving all your land to Job." [Uz smiling nods, 'yes.']

THE HOLY SPIRIT DESCRIBES

UZ: A few days later Uz takes his son camel riding and at the top of the hill speaks,"Job, an angel in a dream spoke to me and said all this land is to be legally 'God's Country' and that I was to 'Will' all this land to you my son. I have reviewed this with your adopted brothers, and your adopted married sisters, who all are becoming very prosperous in the City of Zion, and they have no desire to manage all this land. I am leaving them 24 karat pure bars of gold in my 'Will.'

Therefore, Attorney Whitestone has drafted me a 'Will' and a deed reserving for me a life estate in all this land and by operation of law as all this will be yours upon my death. The camels, the oxen, the sheep, the donkeys, and all this land will be yours to hold in trust for the Lord's use. With the servants and a Stewart, you could manage this from Zion if you had rather live there.

The land should adequately support itself unless you had a major disaster. I remember that dream about how happy you were practicing law and how the Lord would use you. Had you rather been a rancher or a lawyer or both?"

JOB: The young man Job replied, "I acknowledge the Lord in all my ways, and He will direct my path," (See Proverbs 3:5) as I was taught me by my friend, Attorney Whitestone. (A few moments of silence.)

Dad, I would rather be a lawyer like Attorney Whitestone and take *"up the case of the stranger"*(Job 29:16b) helping so many people *'knowing that I had influence in court* (Job 31:21b) with an emphasis also on being like you, a rancher and a farmer on the side. I have been praying for favor with Attorney Whitestone. Would you ask him to train me in jurisprudence? Dad that is what I desire to do! To be a lawyer like Whitestone, and to help others, giving God all the glory. However, I also will manage this land for the glory of God."

UZ: "Start packing! We leave for Attorney Whitestone's law office at Sunrise. I am signing my Will tomorrow, leaving all this to you. You will have to take care of your mother if I should die first. She will make an excellent babysitter for all the grandchildren. Hint! Hint! You can always open a branch law firm here in Uz." [Jumping up and down for joy, Job is speechless.]

Uz laughing, "This is probably the last time you will ever be speechless again as you like Whitestone also have a way with words. Enjoy every moment with Whitestone. True wisdom and riches are knowing God, having joyful contentment in one's lot in life, and in God, one trust. Now have fun and take the time to smell the roses. I give and sing you my son this counsel,

UZ SINGS

'*Don't wear yourself out trying to get rich; have the wisdom to show restraint!*
In the blink of an eye, wealth disappears, for it will sprout wings and fly away like an eagle.' (Proverbs 23:4-5)
Also, remember to acknowledge the Lord in all your ways, and not rely only on your own understanding, and God will direct your path and give you the ultimate success. (See Proverbs 3:5-6) Remember always to give God all the glory with joy and Thanksgivings! '*He who honors the Lord, the Lord will honor.*'(1 Samuel 2:20) It seems you were made to practice law before your birth. It is like you know a lot about jurisprudence, without even studying law."

Job being filled with such contentment and calmness joyfully skips along going to pack. In the morning, before they leave, they walk together man-to-man, father and son, enjoying going through Job's dad's flock of sheep, camels, oxen, and donkeys. Job ponders in his heart what his dad meant by, '*Cast but a glance at riches, and they can be gone.*' (Proverbs 25:5) *I'll never let that happen! With this jump start, I will be the wealthiest in all the land.*"

EDOM: Job's mother, Edom, unsuccessfully seeking to hold back her tears, loads a basket of such delicacies behind Job in the wagon saying, "My son, my only son, God knows how I am going to miss you! Regarding some of the wealthy families who are clients of Whitestone, some of their daughters will see you as a good catch. Remember not all that glimmers may be gold! Marriage is a covenant – until death do you part in this life. You want no wife wanting you dead, so she will inherit your estate and be free from helping you. Marriage can be Heaven on Earth, but if she ever comes to not loving you or the God you serve, or even wishing you dead, it can be most unpleasant. Stay humble my son and acknowledge the Lord and God will have at the end of your life a precious wife, who truly loves you, and will stick and cleave to you, like a cocklebur stuck to your riding coat as you walk through the fields, in both the good times and the bad."

Job bends over and gives his mother a kiss right on the lips and a hug around her neck and turns to the driver saying, "Godspeed!" Job turns back waving at his mother thinking in song,

"I am a good catch. The most handsome, well built, and smartest in the land. No wife would ever want me dead. I will never experience bad times. Why would my mother say such things?"

ADAPTED FROM THE UNABRIDGED
www.amazon.com Books Love & War by Joe Ragland
LOVE & WAR, JOE RAGLAND, AMAZON.COM BOOKS
www.raglandministries.org/loveandwarbook/
BOOK NINE – Chapter 2

Scene Forty-Three

Job Practices Law under Attorney Whitestone's License

,

WHITESTONE: "**Scholar Job, you have** been performing the title abstracting for Grant now for some two years. He is the second largest landowner in Zion. Your dad is the largest. Grant has all the property just north of your father's property. I have bad news – he is dying, as we all must. I quickly prepared a 'Will' for him to sign, but I am scheduled to be in Court today.

His wife has recently died, and his daughter has managed the family affairs for a time. I met briefly once his daughter, Nissa, and I have heard that she is on the wild side and may be looking for a husband she can show off to her friends. Why she would need one, I do not know as she is independent and wants no one to tell her what to do.

I have kept you from meeting her as I felt she was too old and controlling for you. If you marry for money, you earn it! Only the Lord knows the heart, and seductive love on one side often turns into dislike, even hate, wishing the other person was dead. Eve wanted what she did not have, and pulled her husband down with her. It must be loyal and true love from a pure heart.

Take our notary secretary along for the 'Will' signing, and Nissa might not be at home as she often goes camel riding in the afternoon with a girlfriend having a bad reputation. Go in separate carriages so our notary can come back immediately after the signing as she has a family. You must come on back immediately after signing the 'Will' as I have law work on your desk waiting for you. I am on my way to Court!"

THE HOLY SPIRIT DESCRIBES

Job with the notary at his side knocks on Grant's front door with the servant, saying, "Please hurry as he is so short of breath."

JOB: Job enters Grant's bedroom and shakes him, saying, "Grant I have brought a '*Will*' just like you wanted to leave everything to your daughter! Here is our notary, and I need you to sign your name on this line."

NISSA: "You must be Attorney Job here for the 'Will' signing. Let me help you prop him up in the bed." In putting the pillows beneath the upper back of her dad, Nissa's low-cut blouse with no bra opens flashing to Job what his pure eyes have never seen previously, and she intentionally brushes Job's hand giving him a seductive grin.

Job's brow breaks out in a cold sweat as this is the first exposed woman he has ever seen as he was seeking to keep himself pure for marriage. In the confusion, Job asked the notary, "Where is the 'Will?'" With a frown, she tabs the legal folder he is holding under his arm between his right arm and side.

Job opens the folder containing the 'Will' and turns it to the last page pointing with the pen, "Grant, sign here!"

Grant signs his name in large letters, and Job hands the executed 'Will' to the notary, saying, "Please notarize the signature, and place this in Grant's file. I will be along soon as I have on my desk a law-skirmish Whitestone has left for me."

[The notary immediately leaves the room out the front door, returning to the law firm.]

JOB: Job walks out of Grant's bedroom saying to Nissa, "Whitestone has a high regard for Grant. His estate will be yours soon."

NISSA: Nissa responds, "Thank you. I have heard what a great lawyer you are. You probably never lost a case. From the top of that hill let me show you the best view of your dad's land. Lay your coat down on this swing and loosen your bow tie and let us look at your dad's land."
Nissa reached the summit first and reached out her hands and pulls Job up crashing his body into hers.

JOB: Job turned away, looked, and said, "That is the Jordan River running through my dad's land."

NISSA: Nissa corrected him, "The Jordan River is a boundary between our two lands. You own one side, and I own the other, and we meet in the middle, which is a good place to meet. Look, it is almost time for dinner. I asked the servants to set you a place, and we have delicious food prepared."

JOB: Job replied, "I have to go! I am sorrow. Whitestone is expecting me back, and I do have some legal work to do."

NISSA: "I also have some legal papers I wish you would look over advise my dad and me. Look dinner is ready now. Dine with us, review these legal documents, and give us your wisdom – 'yes' or 'no' should we accept this. We need to follow your counsel. Bill us for your expert legal advice. How about a tasty dinner, as you are so thin. When was the last time you had a good meal? Your checks are sucked in from malnutrition.

262

You are so skinny if you were not wearing those suspenders your pants would probably fall off. This tasty nutrition meal would be a step in the right direction to keep you from blowing away."

JOB: "I could always inform my partner Whitestone that Mr. Grant had some legal papers for me to review. I am hungry, as I have not eaten anything today. So I guess it would not hurt."

WHITESTONE: Back at the law office, Whitestone frowns, "Where is Job, as this is not like him? Is he acknowledging the Lord in **all** his ways? (Proverbs 3:5-6) I should have never sent him to the Grants. That daughter is so seductive she even made the hair on the back of my neck stand out that one time I briefly met her. What have I done? I did not myself acknowledge the Lord in **all** my ways in sending him. How could I forget to do that?"

JOB: Back at the candlelight dinner, Job remarks, "It sure is dim in here with just these two candles. You have some excellent cooks. I have never had such a tasty meal. I cannot read your legal papers under these dim candles."

NISSA: Nissa flatters, "I have never had a meal with such a handsome gentleman. Where did you learn such manners? The companionship is delightful. I have the legal papers for you in my dad's private study. I will leave you alone with them and come back in about forty minutes as I would like to change clothes."

Nissa re-enters, wearing a black low cut tight dress with a slit up the side and sits on the corner of her dad's desk showing her legs. Job with another cold sweat on his forehead turns over the last page as he completes his review of the legal documents.

Nissa whispers, "I told the cooks what you said, and they prepared a delicious dessert for us out on the Gazebo up on the hill just in time to view the full moon rising in twenty minutes. 'Yes' or 'no' should I sign this contract? Just a simple 'yes' or 'no' will do for me as I need not know the details."

JOB: Job blushingly nods, '*No.*'

NISSA: Nissa picks up the legal papers and throws them into the trash can and taking Job's arm, promising, "This dessert will be of the gods. I hope you enjoy it and me. The full moon is rising just for us."

Two candles and the most delicious dessert waiting, with no servants in sight, they arrive. Nissa taking charge directs, "Sit here as the full moon will be rising over that hill in about thirteen minutes. I will sit beside you."

JOB: Without having his customary Prayer of Thanksgiving, Job joins Nissa in digging into the desert inquiring, "What is this called? It is delicious! Wow. Nuts. Chocolate. Fudge sauce. I never had anything so tasty."

NISSA: Nissa scoots over with her leg touching Job's leg, smiling replies, "Temptation. It's hard to resist something this tempting."

JOB: Job replied, "I must go!"

NISSA: "No, only six more minutes before the moon rises. It is a tradition around here that when the full moon breaks above the Earth's horizon, you are to kiss on the lips the person nearest to you. We would not want to break that tradition, would we? I cannot kiss myself! You pucker, and I will kiss you. Have you ever been kissed before by a woman?"

JOB: Silence. Job pulls his leg slightly away from Nissa's leg with her quickly closing the gap. At that moment, the light of the full moon breaks the horizon, and as it rises, Nissa turns getting up on her knees facing Job and licking her lips looking over her shoulder saying, "Get ready. Anticipation! Pucker! Let me teach you the best way to kiss a woman. An experience of a lifetime is coming your way." Just as the full moon rising breaks the horizon, Nissa presses her body against Job and passionately kisses him for several minutes. When she broke the kiss, she said, "What did you think of that?"

JOB: "I have to go!"

NISSA: Nissa replied, "Just one kiss is bad luck. Let us try it again!. This time, Job kisses her back on her soft lips, and it felt like smoke was coming out his ears as she pressed her body against his."

She said as Job was preparing to leave, "I do have another set of legal papers I need you to read over. Tomorrow night we are serving quail over wild rice and our moon is still full, and it rises approximately forty-nine minutes and six seconds later tomorrow evening. I have studied the moon times intensely on my roof. The man on the moon and I are friends as he watches over me. Please be here after work for review of the legal papers and dinner. Please!"

JOB: "Okay. Just this one last time."

WHITESTONE: As Job walks into the law firm's conference room the next morning Whitestone frowned with anger, "Job, I waited here for you last evening past midnight. I needed your legal assistance in preparing important legal papers I have to sign under my signature due for filing in Court today. I am off to the court now as I prepared them without your legal assistance.

You are not a lawyer yet! Our notary told me you paraphrase the 'Will,' and you know ethically a 'Will' must be read prior to signing word-by-word. You could have slipped something in on him, which you did not, but this was an ethical violation. Why didn't you come back as I asked you?"

JOB: "Sir, Mr. Grant had other legal papers he wanted me to review."

WHITESTONE: "Are you telling me the whole truth or half-truth?"

JOB: "A half-truth, Sir. His daughter was the one with the legal papers, and I did review them and advised her not to sign them."

WHITESTONE: "How long did that take?"

JOB: "About thirty minutes and then she announced that the dinner was ready and asked me to join her. It was a delicious meal. One of the best I ever had. She has another legal document for me to review, and I agreed to come back this evening and give her my legal opinion."

WHITESTONE: "Job, my son, you are practicing law without a license! That is a crime to which you could go to jail. You are going to get disbarred before you start!"

JOB: "Sir, I think I'm in love with her. It was like love at first sight."

WHITESTONE: "Son, I warned you. She has a seductive spirit about her. It was lust at the first seductive touch of her. The man is the aggressor, and the woman is the responder! You were seduced! Her hook is in your mouth, and she is going to reel you in like a fish. You will be fried in her pan, and your bones will be thrown away when she is through devouring your precious life.

I can send word to her that something has come up, and you can't come this evening and for her to send this so-called legal document to me as you can only review this only under my law license. Remember, you have no authority to practice law on your own! Again, practicing Law without a license is itself a crime!"

265

JOB: "No, I have given my word. Besides that, I need to see Nissa again. I have never met anyone like her. She looks and acts so womanly! She makes me feel like a man."

WHITESTONE: "I made a costly mistake. I could go with you this evening to see my client Grant and to pray for him."

JOB: "Okay. You can go to cover me under your law license, but let us go in separate carriages as I don't want a lecture all the way there and back home. You can come back early, and I will shortly follow you back to the law firm after I briefly talk to Nissa alone about something unrelated to law. Life is not all law!"

THE HOLY SPIRIT DESCRIBES

Whitestone and Job arrive at the Grant home a few minutes early. Whitestone informed the house cleaner, "I am going in to see Mr. Grant. Inform Nissa that his attorney Whitestone has come to pray for her dad and to review the legal document she has. Job will be present, but he is still in training."

The house cleaner showed Whitestone and Job to Mr. Grant's bedroom and indicated that she would inform Nissa they had arrived.

The maid locates Nissa, who was scantily dressed notifying her that Whitestone and Job have arrived.

NISSA: Nissa angrily stomps, "*Damn! I will need to change clothes. He is guarding that soon to be a lawyer – a rich lawyer. I shall not let him get away!*"

WHITESTONE: Whitestone and Job prop Grant's shoulders up on a pillow with Whitestone giving him some water through a straw. Whitestone pulls out the signed 'Will' and reads it word-by-word to Grant asking him whether there might be anyone else he would like to leave some of his great wealth to besides his daughter Nissa. Grant, in a weakened condition, shakes his head no. Whitestone holding his friend's hand sings and prays,

WHITESTONE SINGS IN PRAYER

"Father in Heaven, You have given us both a good life full of years and prosperity. I anoint my brother with oil for his burial, and if he has committed any unforgiven sins, I thank you they are all forgiven. (See James 5:14-15) It is appointed to man once to die and after that the judgment.(Hebrews 9:27) Thank You we both hear those words from You, '*Well done, thou good and faithful servant.*' (Matthew 25:23) '*To be absent from the body is to be present with the Lord.*' (2 Corinthians 5:8) Because of the joy of being in God's presence, '*The day of one's death is better than the day of one's birth.*' (Ecclesiastes 7:1) I know I will see you, Grant, soon. Into God's hands, I commit my friend's spirit. In Your Son's Name, Jesus, whom you revealed to us, we pray. Amen!"

Nissa had walked up standing behind Job wearing a long sleeve, high-top conservative black dress going down to the floor as both she and Job said, 'Amen' to Whitestone's prayer. At that moment, her dad breathed his last. She fell to her left knee faking weeping thinking, *"I'm the richest woman in the world and Job is about to be the richest man in the world when his dad dies. Be good to keep all that wealth in the same family."* Finally, she looked up at Whitestone saying, "You are invited to the funeral service Sunday afternoon at 3:00 P.M. as he requested to be buried here under the oak tree, he loved. I will pay my vows (See Proverbs 7:14) and make a peace offering unto the Lord."

Whitestone, who himself was crying and shaken and hearing the thunder outside, indicated that he would go back, and he directed Job to follow him shortly, with Job also in tears nodding, 'yes.'

JOB: "Nissa, hand those legal papers you want me to look over directly to Mr. Whitestone as I have to review these under his supervision. I will stay here with you a little while as you might need a shoulder to lend on."

Nissa gave the legal papers to Mr. Whitestone on the way to his carriage with sounds of thunder and flashes of lightning in the distance.

WHITESTONE: Whitestone urging, "Son, come on soon before the cold rain starts as you know crossing the creek is dangerous."

JOB: "I'll be along soon."

HOLY SPIRIT DESCRIBES

As Whitestone drove to the end of the road, Nissa puts her head on Job's shoulder saying, "I am so glad you were here when he died. Your dad and Whitestone will be next. Come, let us have a Quail dinner together that my servants have prepared for us."

During the dinner, a violent thunderstorm broke out with torrents of cold rain falling with Job being more-and-more concerned about Whitestone traveling back alone and having to pass through that creek. Finally, the rain stopped, and Job said, "I must go. I must go now!"

With that, Nissa walked Job to his carriage saying, "Thank you for being here. I hope to see you Sunday for the funeral at 3:00."

Job nods a yes and travels the road back. When he got to the Creek swollen with floodwaters, he saw Whitestone's buggy turned over and his horse snorting down at some object. Job ran, and that object was Mr. Whitestone. Job at first thought he was dead, but noted shallow breathing. Job with superhuman strength picks up Mr. Whitestone and lays him in his carriage, ties Whitestone's horse to the rear, and heads to the Doctor's home not far away.

JOB: "Job bangs on the doctor's door saying, "There has been an accident!"

The doctor came to the door in his nightclothes with Job indicating, "It's your friend, Mr. Whitestone. He is still breathing, but barely."

The doctor and Job put warm nightclothes on Whitestone and covered him with blankets. In the morning, Whitestone came to for a few moments coughing with congested lungs, whispering, "Job, I thought I was a goner when that flash flood hit me. Is my horse okay? Look in my top desk drawer for your signed license to practice law as I feel this may be my time to join my friend Grant. I have left everything to you in my Will in the safe. God knows your future, and needs your law license as He has special legal work for you to do for Him. You love God and God loves you. God will save you in the end, and you will see that all things work together for good in your life as you acknowledge the Lord in all your ways. (Proverbs 3:5-6)

You are to love righteousness, and hate wickedness, and your God will set you above your companions and anoint you with the oil of joy and gladness (Psalm 45:7) on Earth and throughout eternity. God gives the best to those who leave the choice to Him! Don't marry Nissa as she does not love God or you!"

After this directive, he went into unconsciousness with his breath and pulse growing weaker and weaker. Job prayed in song for his friend,

JOB SINGS IN PRAYER

"My Father in Heaven, Whitestone has taught me Your truth, honor, ethics, and the law. Into Your hands, I commend his spirit to join his friend Grant. May they both be so blessed in Paradise! [Job thinking, *"Where did the word 'Paradise' come from as it is I have been there before?"*]

'It is appointed unto man once to die (it seems I've lived without ever dying), *after that the judgment.'* (Hebrews 9:27)

If he has committed any sins not confessed, I ask you to forgive! (James 5:15) I pray myself to die *'an old man and full of days.'* (Job 42:17)

In the Name of Your Son, Jesus, who will come and pay the penalty by shedding His life's Blood for the sins of those who will receive Him as Savior. Amen!

With that prayer, Whitestone's breathing became weaker and weaker until he breathed no more. Job told the doctor that Whitestone had indicated that he wanted to be buried under the oak tree on the courthouse lawn, with permission already obtained since he was an officer of the court. Let us have Mr. Whitestone's funeral and burial Saturday afternoon at 3:00 p.m. at the courthouse. I will put a sign on the law office door and pack and head home to my family. Will you please have the grave dug and his body ready for burial in a casket Sunday for me and assure all involved that I will pay them for their labor."

Job drives his carriage to the law firm and opens Mr. Whitestone's desk with tears falling from his eyes as he sees his signed "*License to Practice Law*" dated a few days before.

Job prepares a sign for the law office door.

Attorney Whitestone's Funeral
Courthouse Lawn – Saturday – 3:00 P.M.
Attorney Job will now handle your case.

Job then quickly packs and enters the yard of his folks with tears still streaming down his face with his mother also crying sitting on the porch.

EDOM: "Job what is wrong?

JOB: Wiping tears from his eyes, Job, replies, "Mother my best friend has just gone to Paradise. How I know it is Paradise, I am not sure how I know, but that is where he is. I should be happy for him as he won the certificate of certificates – eternal life with God!

Look, mother, as he opens the folder and shows her his signed *'License to Practice Law.'* I am a lawyer, a member of the Bar of Zion. It was not easy, but I made it. I was indeed trained by the very best! I thank you and dad for giving me a profession so I can help others. Where is dad?"

EDOM: "Son, my only son, your dad is with Whitestone in Paradise, a place you seem to know about as your father died a couple of hours ago. We are going to have the funeral here Friday afternoon at 3:00 P.M. All this is yours, and the servants are going to need to see stability and leadership in you. You can do it!" Job goes into his room, shuts the door, and kneels at his boyhood bed and cries unto the Lord,

JOB SINGS IN PRAYER

"My Father, I know that *'the day of one's death is better for them than the day of one's birth.'* (Ecclesiastes 7:1) The time will come in eternity when, *'God will wipe away every tear from our eyes, and there will be no more death, mourning, crying, or pain because all the old order are gone.'* (Revelation 21:4) Until that glorious time in eternity, help us left on the Earth be tender-hearted and mourn and weep over the death of those we love.

It will happen in the last days, *'There will be more and more evil* (sin; lawlessness in the world), *so most people will stop showing their love for each other* (love of most will grow cold). *But the people who keep their faith* (endure; stand firm, persevere) *until the end will be saved. The Good News* (Jesus, the Son of God, saves) *about God's kingdom will be preached in all the world* (as a witness; testimony of an offer of salvation to be received or rejected) *to every nation. Then the end will come.'* (Matthew 24:10-14)

Use me, Lord Jesus before I die, as I believe You used me in a prior Earth Age, to help prepare the way for the coming of the seed of woman to crush the head of Satan.

Help me take care of mother. Comfort her during this time. May the servants indeed see stability in me. In the Name of Your Son, Jesus. Amen!"

Scene Forty-Four

Job Seduced into Agreeing to Marry an Unbeliever

THE HOLY SPIRIT DESCRIBES

Job going through the loss to death of his best friend and dad desired to say faith-filled words at Mr. Grant's funeral arrives around 2:00 P.M. Sunday going to the large Oak tree and looking at the burial site. He sees Nissa in black watching him. Job's words spoken at the funeral lacked his normal anointed flow of favor. The words he shared about Jesus, the Son of God, at Grant's funeral, fell on deaf ears, being ignored as if he had cast his *'pearls before swine.'* (Matthew 7:6)

JOB: After the funeral Job waives to Nissa declaring, "I must go."

NISSA: "Please stay with me just a little while as I am all alone. Please!"

JOB: "I only have an hour. I must get back to the law office."

NISSA: "Lay your coat down and lose your bow tie. The law business can wait! Let us again walk up to our Gazebo and talk. I am pulling off this hot black outfit as I have something under it more comfortable."

Job sits in his former seat as Nissa crosses and shows her bare sun tanned legs and sitting beside him turns facing him, saying, "Job, just let me lay my head on your shoulder for a few minutes. As he pulls back, she said, I love you! I assure you that our marriage bed will be fun. I have the nicest figure, and it's all yours to enjoy." With that, she pressed her breasts against his chest, rubbing them on him in circles and kissing him until he kisses her back."

JOB: Job explores, "I have always wanted a lot of children. Under the present law of the land if a spouse, such as I was to die all the property owned during the marriage goes to the surviving spouse and the living children equally. If no living children, then all the property belongs to the surviving spouse. I would desire a lot of children for all our land.

NISSA: Nissa smiles, "You do the happy bedroom aggression, and I'll do the happy bearing of children. Deal?"

JOB: Job stands, "Deal. I must get back to the law office."

NISSA: "Let's have a party here Friday evening, and I will invite my best friend, and some of the other prominent wealthy folks and we will publicly announce our engagement. How about June 6th for a wedding right, at 6:00 P.M., here on the grounds and we will make my dad's master bedroom our master bedroom forever. We will make together sweet bedroom music!"

Nissa takes Job by the coat, advancing, "Now you do not run away before I give you a passionate hug and kiss for the road."

Nissa presses her body up against Job passionately kissing him, saying, "There is much more passion ahead. We can have fun, and I will give you a mess of sons and daughters. They will be wealthy at birth, and they will be spoiled being born with a golden spoon in their mouth. I hope you like sexual intimacy, for you can have all you want!"

Nissa takes one of his hands, looking Job in the eyes batting her eyelashes, she places Job's hand over her left breast saying, "Preview of coming attractions. No one has nicer and shapelier breast than I. How do you like them?"

JOB: Swallowing hard, Job, replies, "You won your case! See you Friday evening."

Job's guilty conscience was bothering him, as he had never touched a woman's breast before. Also, it was even his goal to save his first kiss and intimate touch for his wedding night

Job had a hard time sleeping that evening as he had been sexually aroused by a woman for the first time. The next day as he worked on a law case his conscience continued to bother him. Then one of the local landowners, Imrie, running into Job on the street in front of Job's law office utters, "I just received it! Here!"

Job looked at the announcement reading:

Requesting the Honor of Your Presence
Friday Evening, 6:00 P.M.
At the Golden Villa, Enticing Mountain
to Announce the Engagement of
Nissa and Job for a
Friday, June 6th Wedding
6:00 P.M.
Please present this card at the front door.
A goat barbecue and wine tasting party
will follow on the Veranda.
Adults only. No children!

271

Job being speechless turns and goes back to his law office thinking, *"What have I done? I hardly know her, and my law partner warned me about her. I was saving my first kiss for my wedding day. How could I fondle her breast not being married to her?* 'Stolen water is sweet,' (Proverbs 9:17), *but it has a bitter and a guilty feeling in one's stomach."*

Job's afternoon Client also received an invitation to the wedding, and at the conclusion of the consultation spoke,

CLIENT: "Job we all know that Nissa is the prettiest girl around on the outside and is the largest landowner in the county. I had a prospector tell me that he was digging for ore on a hill overlooking her Golden Villa, and two gorgeous women were on the roof sunbathing together naked. He said when they arose they embraced pressing their bare breast against each other and hugged each other's naked bodies, kissed each other with passionate lust, and then went inside."

JOB: Job pointed to the door mandating, "That's hearsay! Say nothing about Nissa again. I will marry the prettiest girl in the county! I believe she is a virgin. Are you coming Friday night?"

CLIENT: "No, I am going to get ready for the Sabbath, which starts for my family and me Friday at Sundown. I do not drink wine as it has ruined so many. My dad was an alcoholic, and if I ever take a sip, I suspect I too could turn quickly into an alcoholic. I would be a goner! A drunkard *'can not please God'* (Romans 8:8), and *'they cannot inherit the Kingdom of God.'* (1 Corinthians 6:10) I have one purpose in life, and that is to please God! Therefore, I stay far away from liquor. Are you going to drink all those sample wines?"

JOB: "No, friend, I do not drink either. I forgot about the Sabbath when I gave her the green light for Friday night. You are right. The only thing that matters is a life pleasing to God! Why should we go through life accomplishing things that in Eternity amount to nothing? Where did that come from?"

THE HOLY SPIRIT DESCRIBES

Friday evening Job arrives at the Golden Villa standing in line with the door attendant taking up the invitations with Job being stopped having none.

NISSA: Nissa was laughing with her girlfriend at the bottom of the stairs both already drinking a second glass of wine screams in a loud voice, "He's the groom - let him in!"

Job looks over and sees Nissa dressed in a black high top dress going all the way to the floor with a slit up the side revealing a tanned leg. By her side, dressed someone like a prostitute in a revealing red dress with high heels, was a female giving Job an uncanny eye.

272

Nissa speaks as Job humbly approaches, "Darling, let me introduce you to Lesba, my very best friend. We went through puberty together."

"Lesba, this is my future husband – June 6th is the big night. Is he not the skinniest thing you have ever seen? He eats and drinks law, forgetting to eat food or drink water. He is so smart, and is a wealthy lawyer!" Nissa focused on her front door seeking to listen what the two women were arguing about to her security officer. Turning back to Lesba inquires, 'Did I tell you he's my lawyer?'"

LESBA: Lesba replies, "Six (6) times now."

NISSA: Nissa proposes, "Darling, Lisba is not married. Perhaps you have a cousin who is also a rich lawyer?" [Women alone laughing as if it was a private joke.]

Nissan takes Job by the arm, saying to Lesba, "Later!"

Nissa walks Job out on the Veranda where a band is playing with people dancing and drinking wine. A pit has on it a freshly killed young male goat cooking in its mother's milk (The prohibition to not cook a young goat in its mother's milk appears three times in the Hebrew Bible: Exodus 23:19, Exodus 34:26, and Deuteronomy 14:2), with blood dripping down into the boiling pan of milk. Another goat soaking in a large pot of its mother's milk is on a large table, with its greasy flesh, being pulled away with two massive six prong hooked forks.

NISSA: Nissa walks over to the band stage and jumps up on the stage and in a loud voice announces, "We want to announce our upcoming wedding right here at 6:00 P.M. on June 6th in front of all these witnesses. Just remember 666. Here is my "husband to be" Job. Is not he good looking! I want you all to come by here and introduce yourself to him. He is a lawyer! He is now your lawyer. After you have met, go to the buffet and enjoy, especially the tasty young goat cooked in its mother's milk and an evening of dancing and wine tasting."

Nissa then introduces Job with much pride and bragging words to many guests who had lined up to meet him. Several guests were seeking Job's answers to various legal questions.

JOB: Job indicates to Nissa after he had met the last guest, "I have the worst headache I've ever had. I never get headaches. God said we are not to cook a young goat in its mother's milk (Exodus 23:19), and the fumes from that awful cooking smell have made me sick."

NISSA: "Drink some of the vintage wine as it will ease your stomach."

JOB: "I don't drink wine. I will go home, take something for this headache, and see if I can sleep it off. Also, I need to cease from my law occupation for today and prepare my soul for the Sabbath as I have been asked to present a devotional in an assembly in the synagogue tomorrow. I encourage you Nissa get ready to, "Remember the Sabbath day, to keep it holy." (Exodus 20:8)

I work six days a week and honor the Lord, my God, and on the seventh day, I rest from working on legal matters in my business. I am leaving now to prepare to honor God through the holiness of being still and worshipping God on the Sabbath tomorrow."

NISSA: Nissa at the carriage looking around and seeing no one watching thinks, *"A headache or no headache here is a special kiss."* While kissing Job, she again takes his hand and puts it over her left breast saying, "These are yours wholly and exclusively! You will have fun. June 6th is right around the corner. A Friday wedding at 6:00 P.M., the six (6) month, and the six (6) day. As for the next day, a Saturday, I remind you that sex isn't working." [Nissa smirks with a seductive smile.]

Nissa not even watching Job drive away gulps from her large glass of wine and walks through a side door back into the Golden Villa. Seeing Lesba at the bottom of the steps, smiling Nissa says with a drunken slur and a gas belch, "Mission accomplished! Come into my parlor says the spider to the rich fly, and we will have gorgeous and spoiled rich baby spiders or something like that."

LESBA: Lesba proposes, "You are getting tipsy. Would you like to go up on the roof to our particular spot? We could get some moon tan and sleep in each other's arms until dawn."

NISSA: Nissa replied, "Why not? I am practically a married woman! I need a fling of fun with my best friend. Let me grab two jugs of wine and we will have a private party. This way I will not have to tell the guest why Job had to leave. They will assume we are romancing somewhere. They will all just leave."

Nissa and Lesba enter the roof garden, and Nissa locks the gate behind them. The full moon rises, giving everything a golden glow. Nissa proclaims, "The 'Golden Village' has turned to gold tonight. Even the gods have sent this moonshine. Look, the man in the moon is smiling down on us. He must be a god. I worship you man in the moon. I can see you, but I cannot see the God of Job. If I can't see it as far as I am concerned, it does not exist." Let us sing our theme song,

NISSA AND LESBA SING

"Hotty Toddy, Man in the Moon almighty,
Who the hell are we, Hey!
Flim Flam, Bim Bam
Female lovers, by damn!

Job's land shall be our land.
His children our children.
Until death, we part as we tie a tight marriage knot.
He shall die first, and we will inherit it all.

LESBA: As your maid of honor, I will help you reel this fish in and skin him. You can cook him in the frying pan with lard, swine's grease, yourself. Until then, let us drink the moonshine!"

Nissa and Lesba pass out drunk in each other's arms as a thick dark cloud covers the light reflected from the moon with Job on his way home shivering as a cold chill goes through him in the darkness.

ADAPTED FROM THE UNABRIDGED
www.amazon.com Books Love & War by Joe Ragland
www.raglandministries.org/loveandwarbook/
BOOK NINE – Chapter 4

Scene Forty-Five

THE HOLY SPIRIT DESCRIBES

Job's Wedding and Honeymoon

Following the wedding, the guest threw black corn seed, and the coachman drove to a private honeymoon condo having a romantic view owned by one of Job's clients.

NISSA: As they arrived, Nissa walked over to the honeymoon bed, turning it down, saying, "Why don't you freshen up with a shower and slip in here and then I will come. Anticipation!" Nissa walked out on the terrace, while Job showered, saying to herself, "*We have a covenant until death do we part. He will die first! He is expecting a virgin. What can I tell him about my not being a virgin? I've got it.*" Nissa comes out of the shower, walking up to the bed expounding, When I was young, my favorite sport was camel racing on the goat trail. Some turns on the narrow goat path have potential falls over the edge into the deep canyon below, which would mean instant death, but it was so exciting. The camels loved it too.

Nissa with two fingers crossed behind her back continues, "One day when I was leading the race, a viper struck at my camel, and my camel threw me off. I fell for some distance hitting my private as I straddled a tree root, which saved my life. Blood was going everywhere as it partially broke my hymen. Someone threw me down a rope and pulled me up. I was somewhat a Tomboy. I was in so much pain and was stove up for days."

Uncrossing the two fingers behind her back, she concludes, "So that is the story of why I have no full intact 'woman's hymen,' just a little part hanging as a 'Chad.' Who knows, I might bleed a little from the 'hanging Chad.' You can totally remove it this evening yourself. I assure you I have never had a man inside me. Let us have fun! No birth control for us."

The next morning Nissa left a note, "*I have taken a walk. Plenty of fruit in the cooler.*"

Job pulls back the top sheet looking for any evidence on the bottom sheet of any bleeding and finding a little red from ketchup, Nissa had added to deceive her husband.

JOB CHANTS

"*Nissa is my wife now. I coveted for better or for worse and until death do us part. I guess some women lose their hymen in accidents. I will give her the benefit of the doubt. I hate that tree that took her virginity. May Nissa personally break that tree off flat to the ground. Lord, I forgot to 'acknowledge You'* (Proverbs 3:6) *in all this. I guess I was on my own not bringing God into this marriage. I so much desire to please You! You know Nissa had me going and I sort of feel like I washed my feet with my socks on.*"

ADAPTED FROM THE UNABRIDGED
www.amazon.com Books Love & War by Joe Ragland
www.raglandministries.org/loveandwarbook/
BOOK NINE – Chapter 5

Scene Forty-Six

Job's Seven Sons, Three Daughters, and Wife Die

THE HOLY SPIRIT DESCRIBES

Job's law practice and land holdings, great wealth, integrity, and that he feared God made him the '*greatest man among all the people of the East*.' (Job 1:3) Few enjoyed the intimacy in marriage as much as Job. His wife kept her promise never to turn Job down when he needed intimacy. Job would laugh joking, "Once a king always a king, but once a knight (night, having intimacy) is enough." Such satisfying intimacy made Job feel even more like a man. Job would travel to his law practice at dawn and would often return home late with Nissa's cook saving him a leftover plate for dinner.

Nissa raised their children, introducing her sons and daughters to the great wealth of producing vintage wines. She allowed their daughters to sunbath naked with her with Lisba joining them on the roof of the villa. She would caution them that this is our womanly secret not to be mentioned to your brothers or your dad. Each of her daughter's discovered Lesba's secrets and were inflamed with lust for one another (Romans 1:21-31) choosing of their own free will to lose their virginity, instead of saving their virginity for marriage as Job had often instructed them to do in his Sabbath Day messages. Nissan would urge Job to focus on his growing and prosperous law practice and leave the daily rearing of the children to her.

Nissa's oldest son had an elaborate black stone house where they often feasted on swine flesh and drank wine boasting in great pride they were gods and invisible. The seven sons had conspired to buy up vineyards, wine presses, and with the means, justifying the ends would drive competitors out of business. The sons obtained a monopoly with excessive profits in wine production and distribution, which resulted in increasing sin and unemployment in Zion. The sons were effeminate, not desiring wives, and the daughters had no desire to submit to or obey husbands.

THE SPIRIT OF TRUTH SINGS

'*In the land of Uz there lived a man whose name was Job. This man was blameless and upright; he feared God and shunned evil. He had seven sons and three daughters, and he owned seven thousand sheep, three thousand camels, five hundred oxen and five hundred donkeys, and had a large number of servants. He was the greatest man among all the people of the East.*

His sons used to take turns holding feasts in their homes, and they would invite their three sisters to eat and drink with them. When a period of feasting had run its course, Job would send and have them purified. Early in the morning, Job would sacrifice a burnt offering (shed innocent blood seeking to cover their sins) for each of them, thinking, 'Perhaps my children have sinned and cursed God in their hearts.' (Job 1:1-5)

FATHER: The Father God said to His Son, Jesus, "Job is shedding the innocent blood of animals seeking to cover the sins of his children, but they have a part to play. You will shed Your innocent blood to pay the penalty for sins for all those who receive You as Savior, repent of their sins, and confess You as Lord.

Job is doing what he can and is seeking to honor You, but his wife and children who have 'free wills' have to overcome, repent, and ask forgiveness of sins.
"

THE HOLY SPIRIT DESCRIBES

SATAN: The prideful fallen angel, Apollyon Lucifer, now Satan called the devil, was so jealous of the beauty of Eve and is now so jealous of the wealth of Job. Satan encountered Gabriel, who was delivering a message to the Earth, probing, "Gab, when do the ministering angels assigned to the Earth present their reports to the Son of God?"

GABRIEL: "The next meeting on Earth with the Son of God is for 3:00 P.M. on the dome of the rock on August 7th in Jerusalem."

SATAN: I plan to attend to make a formal legal objection about this Job fellow on this issue, 'Does Job fear God for nothing?' (Job 1:9)

FATHER: "Son and Holy Spirit, Lucifer is legally now Satan and received limited legal authority in the Planet Earth after Adam chose to obey him over Us. Adam legally gave to the devil a portion of his lease to the Earth. Now Satan will contend that if he can be allowed to turn the heat up on Job, he can like he so easily did with Adam, get Job to obey him and not to trust Us. I believe Job, made in Our image, is man enough after having done all necessary *'to stand against the wiles of the devil.'* (Ephesians 6:11) Job will look Satan in the eye and never back up! A man's man, *'after My own heart, who will do everything I want him to do!'* (Acts 13:22)

THE SPIRIT OF JESUS SINGING

'One day the angels came to present themselves before the Lord (Jesus), and Satan also came with them. The Lord said to Satan, 'Where have you come from?'
Satan answered the Lord, 'From roaming through the Earth and going back and forth on it.'
Then the Lord said to Satan, 'Have you considered my servant Job? There is no one on Earth like him; he is blameless and upright, a man who fears God and shuns evil.

'Does Job fear God for nothing?' Satan replied. 'Have You not put a hedge around him and his household and everything he has? You have blessed the work of his hands, so his flocks and herds are spread throughout the land. But stretch out Your hand and strike everything he has, and he will surely curse you to Your face.'

The Lord said to Satan, 'Very well, then, everything he has, is in your hands, but on the man himself do not lay a finger.'

Then Satan went out from the presence of the Lord.' (Job 1:6-12)

FATHER: "Son, the devil is a destroyer, liar, and a murderer. Legally the time will come when Michael will throw him into a lake of fire to be no more. He is Our first creation and has certain legal rights, but when he murders an innocent man, You, My Son, His punishment will fit the crime. Let us pick up here,

'One day when Job's sons and daughters were feasting and drinking wine at the oldest brother's house, a messenger came to Job, and said, 'The oxen were plowing, and the donkeys were grazing nearby, and the Sabeans attacked and carried them off. They put the servants to the sword, and I am the only one who has escaped to tell you!'

While he was still speaking, another messenger came and said, 'The fire of God (unknown to Job this was lightning sent from Satan) fell from the sky and burned up the sheep and the servants, and I am the only one who has escaped to tell you!'

While he was still speaking, another messenger came and said, 'The Chaldeans formed three raiding parties and swept down on your camels and carried them off. They put the servants to the sword, and I am the only one who has escaped to tell you!'

While he was still speaking, yet another messenger came and said, 'Your sons and daughters were feasting and drinking wine at the oldest brother's house, when suddenly a mighty wind swept in from the desert and struck the four corners of the house. It collapsed on them, and they are dead, and I am the only one who has escaped to tell you!"

At this, Job got up and tore his robe and shaved his head. Then he fell to the ground in worship (of God) and said:

'Naked I came from my mother's womb, and naked I will depart. The Lord gave, and the Lord has taken away (he did not realize that it was the Lord's enemy, who had come to steal, kill, and destroy and that the Lord allowed it to test Job's trust and faithfulness); *may the name of the Lord be* (blessed) *praised.'*

In all this, Job did not sin by charging God with wrongdoing.' (Job 1:13-22)

FATHER: "My Son, Job, rightly feared his children sinning against and cursing Us (going to Hell when they died) as they loved their wine, swine's flesh, and parties speaking proud boasting words, often using Our names in vain in their jokes and jesting. They each bragged they were self-made and would live their life their own way and not God's way as urged by Job. They countered that it was their life, and chose to spend their wealth doing fun things. Although they became utterly unteachable, Job admonished them to choose righteousness, to honor and acknowledge Us, with them mocking and laughing that they would enjoy the pleasures of sin for a season and repent on their deathbed. They gave Satan a place, and he killed them in six seconds with a tornado. Satan timed each of these disasters seeking to cause Job to curse Us and hopefully die and be a trophy for him in Hell. Job's children died in their sins and all ten, including his three beautiful non-virgin daughters, later were joined by their mother in Hell, with Satan smirking and gloating.

Notwithstanding, Job resigned himself to Our will being done, which We allowed to take place, no matter what it would cost him even if it were everything. Job was willing to march into Hell for a Heavenly cause and never back up. He had that shadow of choosing again to give it all away in the First Earth Age and here he is again in the Second Earth Age bringing all this land together in one mass for Zion. He rightly recognized that all his blessings since his birth have come from Us.

Job in the First Earth Age gave all his land for Our Kingdom business. Job will again give all his land in this Second Earth Age for Our Kingdom business! Job will reap the greatest blessings possible for a flesh and blood man to receive on Earth. Job will look evil in the eye and never back up as he walks in love and carries a big stick (offensive weapon) being the Word of God.

Job's subconscious has shadows of his life as a lawyer in the First Earth Age. He only subconsciously knew it was not Us stealing from him, but the attack against him is from the one who destroyed the Earth in the First Earth Age. His words proved that he did not serve Us because of the prosperity he received. Job wins round one as Satan has made a false accusation against Job and Us. Here comes the defeated accuser of the saints back to You again for another attack against Job,

SPIRIT OF JESUS SINGS

'On another day the angels came to present themselves before the Lord, and Satan also came with them to present himself before Him. And the Lord (Jesus) said to Satan, 'Where have you come from?' Satan answered the Lord, *'From roaming through the Earth and going back and forth in it.'*

Then the Lord (Jesus) said to Satan, *'Have you considered my servant Job? There is no one on Earth like him; he is blameless and upright, a man who fears God and shuns evil. And he still maintains his integrity, though you incited Me against him, too* (permit you to seek to) *ruin him without any reason.'*

'Skin for skin!' Satan replied. *'A man will give all he has for his own life. But stretch out your hand and* (allow me to) *strike his flesh and bones, and he will surely curse You to your face.'*

The Lord said to Satan, *'Very well, then, he is in your hands, but you must spare his life.'* (Job 2:1-6)

So Satan went out from the presence of the Lord and afflicted Job as it is written and sung,

THE SPIRIT OF TRUTH SINGS

'So Satan afflicted Job with painful sores from the soles of his feet to the top of his head. Then Job took a piece of broken pottery and scraped himself with it as he sat among the ashes.' (Job 2:7-8)

NISSA: His wife (Nissa) said to Job, '*Are you still holding on to your integrity?* **Curse God and die!**' (Job 2:9)

JOB: '*You are talking like a foolish* (ungodly) *woman. Shall we accept good from God, and not trouble* (Job did not know it was the devil)*?*'
In all this, Job did not sin in what he said (He spoke nothing with a judgmental or critical motive about the God he loves).' (Job 2:10)

NISSA: "God so afflicts you that you are too far gone to recover, and you are about to die. I bore you ten children. Your God murdered them, and is close to murdering you! Now curse your evil God and die. (Job 2:9) How can you have trust in a God who would inflict you like this? I will curse God for you!

I am going camel racing with Lisba. The loser must give the other an imported skin of the highest quality Egyptian vintage wine for us all to enjoy. If I win, I will bring you my wineskin as this would be a good time for you to start drinking to help forget your troubles. Now curse your unreasonable God and die. The sooner, the better for all of us!"

JOB: "Darling don't be so foolish as to go camel racing on that narrow goat trail. What would I do without you? I love you so much. I will not drink that wine, but '*instead I will be filled with the Holy Spirit*!' (Ephesians 5:18) Don't bring it into our house!"

NISSA: "Don't tell me what to bring into my house. I am the captain of this castle, and I allow you to stay in my eloquent master bedroom. You might return to your mother's home as I cannot bear to look at you or smell your breath anymore. I am in control here! Now curse God and die as God has just about killed you!"

JOB: "God has not forsaken me. He is allowing all this to happen for the eternal good of His Kingdom. '*No weapon formed against me will prosper.*' (Isaiah 54:17) I am still breathing God's air, walking on God's Earth, and I feel I still have a few friends left, although many are deserting me. I speak the truth that my God is good and, in the end, this will all work for my eternal good and the good of His eternal kingdom. Do not go! I know I look hideous, and my breath smells bad. I do not believe these running sores are contagious to others. Sit with and talk for a while. Stay with me and encourage me just a little as I wait on my God."

NISSA: His wife scoffed, "I'm going to go beat Lisba! We have a bet! Lisba has a special gift for me with a '**P**' on it. Bye!"

THE HOLY SPIRIT DESCRIBES

Job's pain increased into the night, so intense he wished he had never been born. (See Job 3:3) The next day for the first time in his marriage, his wife did not come in during the night. Finally, one of his former clients, Joel, came to see Job, having an extra camel, with Job with tears pleading,

JOB: "Joel, my friend, it is not like Nissa, not to come in last evening. I am concerned that something might have happened to her. Would you loan me your extra camel to allow me to go look for her."

JOEL: Joel with tears for his friend responds, "It is not a loan. It is a gift. You saved me several times from ruin. This camel is my little daughter's pet, Hump, and I am sure she would want me to give it to you. She once dreamed that you had saved her life. She considers you her secret friend and hero. Remember, I once let her come with me to your law office on business. She dresses and acts like a tomboy, but I believe with a miracle from God, she can change and truly be a beautiful lady of God and marry a godly man and give me lovely grandchildren."

JOB: "I receive Hump as a loan. I'll bring him back to you and please thank your daughter for the loan."

JOEL: "I will, My friend, God, can heal those painful sores. Do me a favor. Do not look at yourself in a mirror! Be enthusiastic and faithful to God, and you will accomplish more than any man will in this Earth Age for the glory of God.. You have precious faith and enthusiasm. You just do not know how many people you have helped. Do not give up or quit. Where there is life, there is hope. 'It is appointed unto man once to die, but after that the judgment.' (Hebrews 9:27) I felt I knew you in a prior Earth Age in which we didn't die? Is that possible?" 'For nothing is impossible with the God.' (Luke 1:37)

JOB: "Yes, I too have faint shadows of knowing you and your daughter in a prior Earth Age and in a place called Paradise."

The camel bows down on its front knees, and Job mounts confessing, "Yes, all things are possible with God! I am not quitting and thanks for the encouragement. God bless you and especially protect and bless your daughter as she blooms like a flower into womanhood."

281

THE HOLY SPIRIT DESCRIBES

JOB: Job heads to the goat trail, and as the trail becomes narrow, with a drop off to the rocks below, Job ties his camel and walks. When he comes to the dangerous hairpin curve, he observes both Nissa's and Lesba's camels grazing on some grass. Job calls out,

```
"Nissa, darling, where are you?  Nissa, answer me!"
```

Job looking down to the canyon below seeing black vultures circling. Tears flowing and screaming out,

```
"Nissa, I warned you.  Do not leave me.  I need you.  I am com-
ing down."
```

Job takes the reins of the women's camels tying them to his camels and winds his way down to the rocks below. He drove the vultures away as he in tears, sees, and smells both corpses partially already eaten by the vultures. Nissa's lower lip, left eye, and left breast was eaten away by the vultures. Nissa was grasping a broken glass container with a "P" on the side, and the contents had spilled out. As Nissa's camel bowed on its front knees beside Nissa's body, Job pulls her body off of a tree broken off at the root, and positions her corpse between the two humps balancing her so she would not slide off. He did the same for Lesba and rode back on Hump shedding many tears with the camel train pulling into the Golden Villa.

It was late when Job arrived back home. Job went to the servant's quarter awakening his trusted servant falling on his neck, crying like a baby whispering, "It is Nissa. She is dead. She fell off
```
the goat trail at the dangerous hairpin.  I told her not to go!
One of you take Lesba's corpse on her camel to her mother.  I do
not want her buried here!  I believe everything I was warned
about Lesba is true.  If it were not for her evil influence, my
Nissa would be alive.  What am I going to do without Nissa?
Build a casket, which we will need to keep shut as part of her
beautiful face was eaten away by vultures.  I desire her to have
a proper burial here on the grounds she loved so much.  Maybe un-
der the Weeping Willow tree as she has brought such sorrow and
weeping.  I was brought low today!  I wonder if I will ever stop
crying?"
```

JOB'S LAMENT SONG AND PRAYER

I am mourning the death of my wife day and night.
Why did she rebel and be no more on the Earth.
Lord, it seems impossible to recover from this grief.
Still, nothing is impossible with the Lord.
I know I have the Kingdom of God business to accomplish.
Lord, help me run Your straight and narrow race for Your glory!
Respectfully asking, my Father God, in the name of Jesus,
Your Son, my Savior and Lord.

ADAPTED FROM THE UNABRIDGED
www.amazon.com Books Love & War by Joe Ragland
www.raglandministries.org/loveandwarbook
BOOK NINE – Chapter 6

Scene Forty-Seven

Attorney Job Buries Wife and Has a Dream

THE HOLY SPIRIT DESCRIBES IN SONG

Following the private burial of Job's wife Nissa, Job was looking the essence of death, with itchy painful running sores all over his body,

` After this, Job opened his mouth and spoke of the day of his birth, and sing,

JOB SINGS

'May the day of my birth perish, and the night it was said, 'A boy is born!' That day – may it turn to darkness; may God above not care about it, may no light shine on it. May darkness and a deep shadow claim it once more; may a cloud settle over it; may blackness overwhelm its light. That night (I was born) *– may thick darkness seize it; may it not be included among the days of the year nor be entered in any of the months.'* (Job 3:1-6)

That night lightning struck the bureau of vital statistics a few yards from Job's Law office with stored oil being ignited into a ball of flame exploding the building into ashes. Then a flash flood overflowing from the nearby river washed all the ashes away as torrents of rain flooded the area. All the recorded documents, including Job's birth certificate and other writings about Job, were all gone from the face of the Earth. The next morning Job was considering the loss of the country records confirming Job's words the night before.

JOB SINGS IN SELF PITTY

'What I feared has come upon me; what I dreaded has happened to me. I have no peace, no quietness; I have no rest, but only turmoil.' (Job 3:1-3, 25-16)

"The day of the recording of my birth is now gone. I cannot even prove who I am except for my license to practice law. I had feared my children would die drinking wine and partying with no fear of God, which happened. I also feared that Nissa would fall off that goat trail and kill herself, which happened just as I spoke out. Nissa is right as I feel like having a numbing drunk, but 'when I became a man, I put childish ways behind me' (1 Corinthians 13:11) *and I will not start drinking now. Nissa, why did you have to die? I warned you. Why did you not listen?*

I am all alone this Friday evening, my special night of romantic fulfillment with my wife. I am burning for romance with Nissa, as she never turned me down when I wanted intimacy. I had 'the natural use of the woman (wife).' (Romans 1:27

With a humble heart, on bended knees, please Lord help me as I am burning for intimacy! Lord, if You were in trouble as I am in trouble and I could, You know I would come to your help, even if it cost me my life! I thought I would be satisfied intimately for life with beautiful Nissa.
   'I humble myself under God's mighty hand, that He may lift me up in due time. I cast all my anxiety (including a burning desire for intimacy) on God because God cares for me.' (1 Peter 5:6-5)

No virgin of Zion would have me as I look and feel the essence of death. I never thought I would ask for help regarding my intense romantic desires awaken by Nissa. I acknowledge You in all my ways to direct my path (Proverbs 3:5-6), *and* 'with a humble heart, on bended knee, please help me!' (*Help Me,* sung by Elvis Presley) *Lord give me the gift of singleness and remove my desire for a virgin wife!"*

THE SPIRIT OF JESUS SINGS TO JOB IN A DREAM

Job laid back and dreamed a dream. In Job's Dream Job heard God the Son, Jesus, answering him,

THE SPIRIT OF JESUS SINGING

"*I will give you* 'a way of escape' (1 Corinthians 10:13). Patience! *Make* 'a covenant with your eyes not to look lustfully at a young woman.' (Job 31:1)

Now remove your wedding ring as it was until death you would part, under the marriage covenant! Help is on the way. Be patient!

Nissa legally forced Me to remove My hand of protection from her and to leave her to her own folly in that dangerous camel race against your advice. Nissa is dead, and you are no longer married!

Here is My promise to you,

'*Now to Him* (Lord Jesus) *who is able to do immeasurably more than all we ask or imagine!*' (Ephesians 3:20)

'And the God of all grace, who called you to His eternal glory in Jesus Christ, after you have suffered a little while, will himself restore you and make you strong, firm and steadfast. To Him be the power forever and ever. Amen.' (1 Peter 5:10-11)

Shalom! Get ready for a surprise blessing!"

284

THE HOLY SPIRIT DESCRIBES

Job awakes with much wonder and amazement, but still in great pain, but with his burning intimacy for Nissa temporality lifted from him!'

Job seeks to remove his wedding ring by pouring on extra virgin olive oil, and finally, with a great effort, it pulls off. Job thought, '*It is easy to put one of these on, but often hard to get it off.*'

Job had a hobby of buying scrap gold, and he goes to his gold crusher and shreds Nissa's wedding ring in it seven times, producing 777 small flakes of 18-karat gold. Job with thanksgiving legally decrees and sings,

JOB SINGS A COVENANT

'*I make a covenant with my eyes*
not to look lustfully (leer) at a young woman.
For what portion should I have from God above,
and what heritage (having the goal to be a joint heir with Jesus)
will I receive from the Almighty on high if I am lewd and immoral?
Does not ruin and calamity (justly) befall the unrighteous?
and disaster the workers of iniquity.
Does not God see my ways and count all my steps
(whether they be moral or immoral)?
(See Job 31:1-4)

ADAPTED FROM THE UNABRIDGED
www.amazon.com Books Love & War by Joe Ragland
www.raglandministries.org/loveandwarbook

BOOK NINE – Chapter 7

Scene Forty-Eight

Job Defends Against the Accusations Hurled Against Him

THE HOLY SPIRIT DESCRIBES

Job draws a crowd as he sits in ashes and *'takes a piece of broken pottery and scraped himself,'* seeking slight relief from the itching and *'painful sores from the soles of his feet to the top of his head'* (Job 2:7). Many expecting and even wishing Job to momentarily die.

The gathering crowd talks about what would happen to his large land holding. Did he have a Will? He has no heirs! Is it contagious? Who will pick him up to bury him? When you lose your health and your family, you lose everything, and the best thing for everyone is for that sick person to die."

Knowing they were talking about such things, Job looked up and waves with his right hand and greets the crowd, "Shalom Y'all. *'My times are in God's hands.'*(Psalm 31:15) God is in control of my life. In God, I trust! I maintain my integrity!"

Job's fellow lawyers and those he called friends, with a mocking look, immediately seeks to condemn and judge Job for advancing his integrity, with accusations and indictments of wrong doing reaping the evil he deserved.

ELIPHAZ ACCUSING JOB CHANTS

`'If someone ventures a word` (showing your wrongdoings) `with you, will you be offended? But who can keep from speaking` (to correct the errors of Job's ways)`? Think how you` (Job) `have instructed many, how you have strengthened feeble hands. Your words have supported those who stumbled; you have strengthened faltering knees. But now trouble comes to you,` *and you are discouraged; it strikes you, and you are dismayed.*

...Consider now: `Who, being innocent, has ever perished?` *Where were the upright ever destroyed? As I have observed,* `those who plow evil and those who sow trouble reap it. At the breath of God, they are destroyed`; `at the blast of His anger they perish.'`

(Job 4:2-5, 7-9)

Job in Shalom (peace) pleads 'not guilty' of such and defends in song,

JOB SINGS IN DEFENSE

'Teach me, and I will be quiet; show me where I have been wrong. How painful are honest words! But what do your (accusing me of wrongdoing) arguments prove?
Do you mean to correct what I say, and treat the words of a despairing man as wind?
You would even cast lots for the fatherless and barter away your friend.
But now be so kind as to look at me. `Would I lie to your face?`
`Relent do not be unjust;` *reconsider,* `for my integrity, is at stake.'`

(Job 6:24-29)

'Is there any wickedness on my lips? Can my mouth not discern malice? ' (Job 6:30)

Therefore, I will not keep silent; I will speak out in the anguish of my spirit, I will complain in the bitterness of my soul." (Job 7:11)

BILDAD AND SHUHITE ACCUSING JOB CHANT

'How long will you (continue to) say such things? Your words are a blustering wind. `God does not pervert justice. Does the Almighty make wrong, what is right? Your children sinned against God, and He gave them over to the penalty` *(of death)* `for their sin.`

But if you will look to God and plead with the Almighty if you are pure and upright, even now He will restore you to your rightful place.' (Job 8:1-6)

JOB FURTHER DEFENDS HIMSELF IN SONG

Job not feeling any guilt or condemnation (See 1John 3:21) for any sins he may have committed, not forgiven, and not knowing it was Satan that had attacked him, defended further,

'God is not human like me (Job) *that I might answer Him. We cannot confront each other in court* (as lawyers).

If only there were someone to arbitrate (as binding legal arbitration settles a matter) *between us, to lay his hand upon us both, someone to remove God's rod from me, so that His terror* (Job didn't know it was Satan attacking him) *would frighten me no more.*

Then I would speak up without fear of Him, but as it now stands with me, I cannot.

(Job 9:32-35)

. . . I loathe my very life; therefore, I will give free rein to my complaint (as a lawyer would present his case) *and speak out in the bitterness of my soul.*

`I will say to God:` `'Do not condemn me, but tell me what charges` (serve me with an indictment, so I will know how to defend myself) `You have against me.`

Does it please You to oppress me, to spurn the work of Your hands, while You smile on the schemes of the wicked?'

. . .You know that I am not guilty and that no one can rescue me from Your hand?

Your hands shaped me and made me. Will you now turn and destroy me?

Remember You molded me like clay. Will You now turn me to dust again?

Did You not pour me out like milk and curdle me like cheese, clothe me with skin and flesh and knit me together with bones and sinews?

You gave me life and showed me kindness, and in your providence watched over my spirit.

But this is what you concealed in Your heart, and I know that this was in your mind:

`If I sinned, You` (God) `would be watching me and would not let my offense go unpunished.`

`If I am guilty - woe to me!` `Even if I am innocent, I cannot lift my head` (to confidentially argue my case as a lawyer), `for I am full of shame and drowned in my affliction.`

If I hold my head high, You stalk me like a lion (Job did not know it was Satan like a roaring lion attacking and seeking to destroy him) *and again display your awesome power against me.*

You bring new witnesses (like presenting evidence in a court of law) *against me and increase Your anger toward me; Your forces come against* (Job did not know it was Satan) *me wave upon wave.*
Why then did You bring me out of the womb? I wish I had died before any eye saw me. If only I had never come into being or had been carried straight from the womb to the grave!

`Are not my few days almost over? Turn away from me so I can have a moment's joy` *before I go to the place of no return* (appointed unto man once to die after that the judgment) . . . . ' (Job 10:1-3, 7-22)

ZOPHAR ACCUSES JOB IN CHANT

Then Zophar the Naamathite further accuse,
'Are all these words to go unanswered? Is this talker to be vindicated?
Will your idle talk reduce men to silence? Will no one rebuke you when you mock?

You say to God, 'My beliefs are flawless, and I am pure in Your sight.'

Oh, how I wish that God would speak, that He would open His lips against you and disclose to you the secrets of wisdom, for true wisdom has two sides.

Know this: God has even forgotten (not true) some of your sins.

. . If He comes along and confines you in prison and convenes a court (as a prosecutor), who can oppose Him?

Surely He recognizes deceitful men, and when He sees evil, does He not take note?

. . . If you put away the sin in your hand and allow no evil to dwell in your tent, and then you will lift up your face without shame; you will stand firm and without fear.

You will surely forget your trouble, recalling it only as waters gone by.

Life will be brighter than noonday, and darkness will become like morning.

You will be secure, because there is hope, and you will look about you and take your rest in safety.

You will lie down, with no one to make you afraid, and many will court your favor.

`But the eyes of the wicked will fail, so they will not escape. Their only hope will be to die.'` (Job 11:1-6, 10-11, 14-20)

JOB PRESENTS HIS DEFENSE IN SONG

Then Job further pleads his case:

`'I have become a laughingstock to my friends, though righteous and blameless!`
. . . To God belong wisdom and power; counsel and understanding are His.
He leads counselors away stripped and makes fools of judges.
He takes off the shackles put on by kings and ties a loincloth around their waist.
He leads priests away stripped and overthrows men long established.
He silences the lips of trusted advisers and takes away the discernment of elders.
He pours contempt on nobles and disarms the mighty.

288

He reveals the deep things of darkness and brings deep shadows into the light.

He makes nations great and destroys them; he enlarges nations and disperses them.

He deprives the leaders of the Earth of their reason; he sends them wandering through a trackless waste.

They grope in darkness with no light; he makes them stagger like drunkards.'
(Job 12:1, 2, 13, 17-25)

'I desire to speak to the Almighty and to argue (as a lawyer) *my case with God. You, however, smear me with lies; you are worthless physicians, all of you!*

If only you would be altogether silent! For you, that would be wisdom.

Hear now my argument; listen to the plea (as a lawyer would plead a case) *of my lips. Will you speak wickedly on God's behalf?*

...Will you argue the case (that God was justified in inflicting me) *for God?*

. . . Keep silent and let me speak; then let come to me what may.

. . . Though He slay me (Job didn't know it was Satan afflicting him with God forbidding Satan to take Job's life), *yet will I hope in God; I will surely defend* (as a lawyer) *my ways to His face.*

Indeed, this will turn out for my deliverance, for no godless man would dare come before Him!

Listen carefully to my words; let your ears take in what I say.

Now that I have prepared my case (as a lawyer), *I know I will be vindicated.*

Can anyone bring charges (as a Grand Jury indictment) *against me? If so, I will be silent and die.*

Only grant me these two things, O God, and then I will not hide from You:

Withdraw Your hand (Job didn't know it was Satan afflicting him) *far from me, and stop frightening me with your terrors.*

Then summon (as into court) *me, and I will answer, or let me speak, and You reply.*

How many wrongs and sins have I committed? Show me my offense and my sin.' (Job 13:3-8, 13, 15-24)

'. . . (A) *man's days are determined* (by God). *You have decreed the number of his months and have set limits he* (the man) *cannot exceed.*

So look away from him and let him alone, till he has put in his time like a hired man.

. . . But man dies and is laid low; he breathes his last and is no more.

. . . If a man dies, will he live again? (Job is having a shadow of eternal life.)

. . . I will wait for my renewal to come.

You will call, and I will answer You; You will long for the creature Your hands have made.

Surely then You will count my steps, but, not keep track of my sin.

My offenses will be sealed up in a bag; You will cover over (forgive) *my sin.'* (Job 14:5-6, 14-17)

ELIPHAZ REPLIES IN CHANT

Then Eliphaz the Temanite replied,
'Your sin prompts your mouth; you adopt the tongue of the crafty (dishonest).
Your own mouth condemns you, not mine; your own lips testify against you.
. . .What is man that he could be pure, or one born of woman, that he could be righteous?
. . . He will no longer be rich, and his wealth will not endure, nor will his possessions spread over the land.
. . . Before his time, he will be paid in full, and his branches will not flourish.'

(Job 15:5-6, 14, 29, 32)

JOB FURTHER DEFENDS IN SONG

Then Job further defends,
'I have heard many things like these; miserable comforters are you all!
Will your long-winded speeches never end? What ails you that you keep on arguing (like a prosecuting attorney)?

Surely, O God, You (Job still unaware this was an attack by Satan) has worn me out, and You have devastated my entire household.

I have sewed sackcloth over my skin and buried my brow in the dust.

My face is red with weeping, and deep shadows ring my eyes, yet my hands have been free of violence, and my prayer is pure.
O Earth, do not cover my blood; may my cry, never be laid to rest!

Even now, my Witness (Jesus, Son of God) is in Heaven; my Advocate (as a lawyer) is on high. My Intercessor (Jesus, Son of God) is my friend as my eyes pour out tears to God; on behalf of a man, He (Jesus, Son of God) pleads with God (the Father) as a man pleads for his friend. (Job 16:1-3, 7, 15-21)

. . . Give me, O God, the pledge you demand. Who else (but Your Son, my Redeemer) *will put up security for me?*

. . . God has made me a byword to everyone, a man in whose face people spit (like God's Son before He died to pay the ransom for the sins of those who would receive Him as Savior and confess Him as Lord)' (Job 17:3, 6)

BILDAD REPLIES IN CHANT

Then Bildad the Shuhite replies,
'When will you end these speeches? Be sensible, and then we can talk.
. . . The lamp of the wicked is snuffed out; the flame of his fire stops burning.
. . . Terrors startle him on every side and dog his every step.
Calamity is hungry for him; disaster is ready for him when he falls.
It eats away parts of his skin; death's (start of wasting away) firstborn devours his limbs.
The memory of him perishes from the Earth; he has no name in the land.

He is driven from light into darkness and is banished from the world.

He has no offspring or descendants among his people, no survivor where once he lived.

Men of the west are appalled at his fate; men of the east are seized with horror. Surely such is the dwelling of an evil man; such is the place of one who knows not God.'

(Job: 18:1-2, 5, 11-13, 17-21)

JOB DEFENDS IN SONG

'How long will you torment me and crush me with words? Ten times now you have reproached me and shamelessly you attack me.

If it is true that I have gone astray, my error remains my concern alone.

Though I cry, 'I've been wronged!' I get no response; though I call for help, there is no justice.

. . His troops (Job does not know it is Satan and his demons at war with him) advance in force.

. . . My kinsmen have gone away; my friends have forgotten me.

. . . My guests and my maidservants count me a stranger; they look upon me (because of the painful sores from the soles of my feet to the top of my head, and my dress is sackcloth covered with ashes) as an alien.

. . . Even the little boys scorn me; when I appear, they ridicule (showing no respect) me.

All my intimate friends detest me; those I love have turned against me.

I am nothing but skin and bones. I have escaped death (in the First Earth Age and to date in the present Earth Age) with only the skin of my teeth.

Have pity on me, my friends, have pity, for the hand of God has struck (didn't know it was Satan) me.

. . . Oh, that my words were recorded, that they were written on a scroll,

I know that my Redeemer (Son of God, who will purchase back those who receive Him as Savior by redeeming them with His own blood) lives and that in the end, He (the Savior) will stand upon the Earth.

And after my skin has been destroyed, yet in my flesh (with a resurrected body of skin and bone) I will see God;

I myself will see Him (God) with my own eyes – I and not another. How my heart wants that to happen!' (Job 19:1-4, 7, 12, 14, 19-21. 23-27)

ZOPHAR REPLIES IN CHANT

Then Zophar the Naamathite replies,

'My troubled thoughts prompt me to answer because I am greatly disturbed.

I hear a rebuke that dishonors me, and my understanding inspires me to reply.

Surely, you know how it has been from of old, ever since man was placed on the Earth, that the pleasures of the wicked are brief, the joy of the godless lasts but a moment.

Though his pride reaches to the heavens, and his head touches the clouds, he will perish forever, like his own dung; those who have seen him will say, 'Where is he?'

Like a dream, he flies away, no more to be found, vanished like a vision of the night.

The eye that saw him will not see him again; his place will look at him no more.

. . .In the midst of his plenty, distress will overtake him; the full force of misery will come upon him.

. . .The Heavens will expose his guilt; the Earth will rise up against him.

291

A flood will carry off his house, rushing waters on the day of God's wrath.

Such is the fate, God allots the wicked, what He had decided they will receive.' (Job 20:1-9, 22, 27-29)

JOB FURTHER DEFENDS IN SONG

Then Job in the style of a lawyer presenting truth continues to defend himself,

'Listen carefully to my words; let this be the consolation you give me.

Bear with me while I speak, and after I have spoken, mock on.

'Is my complaint directed to man? (Job did not know it was Satan afflicting him with God having faith in Job that Job would pass the test.) *Why should I not be impatient?*

Look at me and be astonished (Job looked horrible with sores all over him), *clap your hand over your mouth.*

. . .Why do the wicked live on, growing old and increasing in power?

Yet they say to God, 'Leave us alone! We have no desire to know Your ways.

Who is the Almighty, that we should serve Him? What would we gain by praying to Him?

But their prosperity is not in their own hands, so I stand aloof from the counsel of the wicked.

Yet how often is the lamp of the wicked snuffed out? How often does a calamity come upon them, the fate, God allots in his anger?

How often are they like straw before the wind, like chaff swept away by a gale?

One man dies in full vigor, completely secure and at ease, his body well nourished, his bones rich with marrow.

Another man dies in bitterness of soul, never having enjoyed anything good.

Side by side, they lie in the dust, and worms cover them both.

I know full well what you are thinking, the schemes by which you would wrong me.

So how can you console me with your nonsense? Nothing is left of your answers, but falsehood!' (Job 21:1-3, 6-7. 14-18, 23-28)

ELIIHAZ REPLIES IN CHANT

Then Eliphaz the Temanite replies,

'Can a man be of benefit to God? Can even a wise man benefit him?

What pleasure would it give the Almighty if you were righteous?

What would He gain if your ways were blameless?

Is it for your piety that He rebukes you and brings charges against you?

Is not your wickedness (you must have committed these horrible secret sins) great?

Are not your sins (evil you have done) endless?' (Job 22:1-5)

JOB FURTHER DEFENDS IN SONG

Then Job defends,

'Even today my complaint is bitter, God's hand is heavy

(Job did not know it was Satan attacking him) *in spite of my groaning.*

If only I knew where to find Him (God), *if only I could go to His dwelling!*

I would state my case (as a defense lawyer) *before Him and fill my mouth with arguments.*

I would find out what He would answer me, and consider what He would say.

Would He oppose me with great power? No, He (Job pleads innocent of any great sin) *would not press charges against me.*

. . .God knows the way that I take; when He has tested me, I will come forth as gold (exceedingly blessed and acquitted because my Redeemer lives).

My feet have closely followed His steps; I have kept to His way without turning aside.

I have not departed from the commands of His lips; I have treasured the words of His mouth more than my daily bread.

However, God stands alone, and who can oppose Him? He does whatever He pleases. (Job 23:1-6, 10-13)

. . . Why does the Almighty not set times for judgment? Why must those who know Him look in vain for such days?

. . .There are those who rebel against the light, who do not know its ways or stay in its paths.

When daylight is gone, the murderer rises up and kills the poor and needy; in the night, he steals forth like a thief.

The eye of the adulterer watches for dusk; he thinks, 'No eye will see me,' and he keeps his face concealed.

In the dark, men break into houses (to steal), *but by day they shut themselves in; they want nothing to do with the light.*

For all of them, deep darkness is their morning; they make friends with the terrors of darkness.

God may let them rest in a feeling of security, but His eyes (God sees all) *are on* (all) *their ways.*

For a little while they are exalted, and then they are gone; they are brought low and gathered up like all others; they are cut off like heads of grain.

`If this is not so,` who can prove *(as prosecuting attorney present reliable evidence)* `me false and reduce my words to nothing?'` (Job 24:1, 13-17, 23-25)

BILDAD REPLIES IN CHANT

Then Bildad the Shuhite replies,

`'How then can a man be righteous before God? How can one born of woman be pure` (did not understand that purity comes only by repenting and being cleansed the shed Blood of Jesus)?

. . . If even the moon is not bright and the stars are not pure in His eyes, how much less man, who is but a maggot – a son of man (born in the flesh, as Jesus often called Himself, shedding His precious blood to pay the price for the sin of those who repent and receive Him as Savior), who is only a worm!' (Job 25:4-6)

JOB DEFENDS IN SONG

Then Job defends:

'*Who has helped you utter these words?*

`. . .God spreads out the northern skies` (Job couldn't see the southern skies from the northern hemisphere) `over empty space; He suspends the Earth` (in outer space) `over nothing` (The Earth is not sitting on anything)`.`

. . . Who then can understand the thunder of His power? (Job 26:4, 7, 14)

. . . As surely as God lives, who has denied me justice (Job unaware that the present prosecution was coming from untruths of Satan), *the Almighty, who has made me taste bitterness of soul, as long as I have life within me, the breath of God in my nostrils, my lips will not speak wickedness, and my tongue will utter no deceit.*

`I will never admit you` (my accusers) **`are`** `in the right` (it is because of my sin all this came upon me); `until I die, I will not deny` (like a lawyer in court pleading the Blood of Jesus for righteousness) `my integrity.`

`I will maintain my righteousness` (God declares Job righteous, as He believed [See Romans 4:23-35] God's Son would pay in the full the penalty due for his sins on a cross) *and never let go* (sought to keep himself in the covenant of God by shedding the blood of animals rolling his sins forward until God the Son would come in the flesh and pay the penalty for Job's sin with His own blood) *and will not reproach me as long as I live.*

. . . I will teach you about the power of God and the ways of the Almighty; I will not conceal.

You have all seen this yourself. Why then this meaningless talk?

Here is the fate, God allots to the wicked, and the heritage a ruthless man receives from the Almighty:

. . . Though he heaps up silver like dust and clothes like piles of clay, what he lays up the righteous will wear, and the innocent will divide his silver.

293

. . . He lies down wealthy, but will do so no more; when he opens his eyes, all (his wealth) is gone. ' (Job 27:1-6, 11-17, 19)

. . . God said to the man, 'The fear of the Lord – that is wisdom, and to shun evil is understanding! '(Job 28:28)

. . . How I long for the months gone by, for the days when God watched over me when His lamp shone upon my head and by His light I walked through darkness!

Oh, for the days when I was in my prime when God's intimate friendship blessed my house when the Almighty was still with me, and my children were around me when my path was drenched with cream, and the rock poured out for me streams of olive oil.

When I went to the gate of the city and took my seat in the public square, the young men saw me and stepped a side, and the old men rose to their feet (such respect); *the chief men refrained from speaking and covered their mouths with their hands; the voices of the nobles were hushed, and their tongues stuck to the roof of their mouths.*

Whoever heard me spoke well of me, and those who saw me commended me because I rescued the poor (as a lawyer coming to their defense) *who cried for help, and the fatherless who had none to assist him.*

The man who was dying(in his last breaths), *blessed me!*

I made the widow's heart sing (by assuring her protective justice).

I put on righteousness as my clothing,
    justice (as a lawyer) *was my robe and my turban.*

I was eyes to the blind
    and feet to the lame.

I was a father to the needy!
    I took up the case (as a lawyer in court) *of the stranger.*

I broke the fangs of the wicked
    and snatched the victims from their teeth.

I thought, 'I will die in my own house,
    my days as numerous as the grains of sand.

 My roots will reach to the water,
    and the dew will lie all night on my branches.

My glory will remain fresh in me,
    the bow ever new in my hand. '

Men listened to me expectantly,
    waiting in silence, for my (legal) *counsel.*

After I had spoken, they spoke no more,
    my words fell gently on their ears.

They waited for me as for showers
    and drank in my words as the spring rain.

When I smiled at them, they scarcely believed it,
    the light of my face was precious to them.

I chose the way for them and sat as their chief.
        I dwelt as a king among his troops.
        I was like one who comforts mourners. (Job 29:2-25)
        But now they mock me,
        men younger than I,
        whose fathers I would have disdained
        to put with my sheep dogs.

. . . And now their sons, mock me in song!
        I have become a byword among them.

They detest me, and keep their distance,
        they do not hesitate to spit in my face.

Now that God has (Job did not know it was Satan) *unstrung my bow and afflicted me,*
        they throw off restraint in my presence.

. . . I have become a brother of jackals, a companion of owls.

My skin grows black and peels (inflicted by Satan);
my body burns with fever (infection).

My harp is tuned to mourning,
        and my flute to the sound of wailing. ' Job 30:1, 9-11, 29-31)

Job Returns to the back bedroom in His Law Firm.

Job continues looking the essence of death with his skin covered with such black, yellow, and red sores with such pain and itching. He continued to scrape himself with pottery causing peeling and the breaking of blood vessels and giving him only minor relief.

Job in pain finally falls asleep. Job dreams about Nissa, who had her with their seductive saying, "Once a king always a king, but once a knight (intimacy once a night) is enough." In his dreams, he missed that nightly intimacy with her as she was a warm and beautiful woman. The intimacy with her gave him such a feeling of manliness with a clear mind the next day, being one of his secrets of having a bounce in his steps and a song in his heart.

Job, especially in his dreams was still romantically burning for Nissa. When he would awake, he would look over at her place in the bed and her pillow beside him, but on the surface of the Earth, she was no more. This burning in his dreams was like a throne in the flesh, and Job asked the Lord now this third time to remove it and give him the gift of singleness. The Lord responded, '*My grace is sufficient for you, for My power is made perfect in weakness.*' (2 Corinthians 12:9) What was Job going to do with a town full of virgin young women with his appearing so hideous?

Some of the prideful young girls when passing Job on the street took delight in mocking him saying such things as, "You stink! You are a skinny worm, not a man. No female would ever touch you. You are a has been! Your appearance would gag a maggot! Job had remembered what would be written of the Son of God, Jesus,

'*But I am a worm* (suffering of Jesus, with His glory to follow) *and not a man, scorned by everyone, despised by the people.*' (Psalm 22:6)

Job had kept himself a virgin until his honeymoon night when Nissa awakened that sleeping tiger of intimate desire in him. Job had been so diligent to guard himself to not undress a young woman with his eyes, keeping his marriage covenant pure with Nissa, until death they parted. But now in bed alone at night, the intimate desire in him often would burn as he thought back to the releases he received with Nissa, who never turned him down even once for intimacy.

One evening after a dark, heavy downpour of rain, Job received a knock on the door of his law firm. When he opened the door, he saw three teenage girls who stepped in with their tops soaked with water wearing no bras, through which one could see well the seductive shapes of their breasts. Job looking them in the eyes only asking, "What do you three want? Who are you?"

NICOLAITAN: The leader responded, "I am Nicolaitan, (see "Nicolaitans" mentioned in Revelation 2:7), and we are from the temple of Balak, (for example, see Revelation 2:14), and we have been sent by Balaam himself and one of your generous admirers to give you some sexual relief. It must be hard being a widower. You must be about to explode. The younger one here is a virgin, and you can have her first. We will leave early in the morning after you have had your fill of the great pleasures we can give you."

JOB: Job looks up to the ceiling ordering, "Out! I said, out!"

Job opens the door with the girls not budging. He then went over to them and not looking at them physically having to throw each girl out the door.

Two men passing by scream out at Job,

"What are you doing to these temple prostitutes? If you don't want them, we will take them."
When the last one landed on the ground, Job declared,

"Repent! God loves you and does not desire you to go to Hell! Never come back here or I will obtain a court order against you. That was not a friend of mine who sent you. That was a child of the devil for the 'sexually immoral' will not inherit (See Revelation 20:7-8) the Kingdom of God. Tell him to repent too, or he will also end up in Hell."

Job slams and locks the door and sweating like drops of blood from the temptation and going over to his desk, he wrote.

"I, Job, at this moment affirm my 'covenant *with my eyes not to ever look lustfully at a girl*.' (See Job 31:1.)

Job bowed and prayed, "Father, please take this strong intimate desire for Nissa away from me. It is a thorn in my flesh. Just give me the gift of singleness! Why did Nissa have to die? She knew how to satisfy me romantically, except she stopped kissing me as she would turn her lips away in lovemaking. Notwithstanding, I never lacked any natural romance as I was so satisfied. Help me!

God, if You were in trouble as I am in trouble, I would help You. You know I would help. You are the One, who invented sexual release in marriage. Help me. I am burning. In Your Son's Name, Jesus, I pray. Amen!"

The next Sabbath after the two men had spread the slander about seeing Job with the temple prostitutes throughout the community, with many in the congregation shaking their heads in disgust at Job.

JOB: Job again stands to defend his innocence before his accusers,

"'*I made a covenant (of purity) with my eyes*
  not to look lustfully at a girl.
For what is man's lot from God above,
  his heritage from the Almighty on high?
Is it not ruin for the wicked,
  disaster for those who do wrong?
Does He not see my ways
  and count my every step?
If I have walked in falsehood
  or my foot has hurried after deceit –
  let God weigh me in honest scales
    and He will know that I am blameless –
  if my steps have turned from the path,
  if my heart has been led by my eyes,
  or if my hands have been defiled,
  then may others eat what I have sown,
  and may my crops be uprooted.
If my heart has been enticed by a woman,
 or if I have lurked at my neighbor's door (to commit adultery with his wife),
 then may my wife grind another man's grain (commit adultery against me),
  and may other men sleep with her.
For that (adultery) *would have been shameful,*
  a sin to be judged.
It is a fire that burns to Destruction (Hell itself),
  it would have uprooted my harvest.
If I had denied justice to my menservants,
  and maidservants
when they had a grievance against me,
what will I do when God confronts me?
  What will I answer when called to account?
Did not He who made me in the womb make them?
  Did not the same One form us both within our mothers?
If I have denied the desires of the poor
  or let the eyes of the widow grow weary,
  if I have kept my bread to myself,
    not sharing it with the fatherless –

. . ., if I have seen anyone perishing for lack of clothing,
    or a needy man without a garment,
and his heart did not bless me
    for warming him with the fleece from my sheep,
     if I have raised my hand against the fatherless, knowing I had influence in court (as a lawyer),
    then let my arm fall from the shoulder, let it be broken off at the joint.
For I dreaded destruction from God,
    and for fear of His splendor, I could not do such things.
If I have put my trust in gold
    or said to pure gold, 'You are my security,'
if I have rejoiced over my great wealth,
    the fortune my hands had gained,
if I have regarded the sun in its radiance
     or the moon moving in splendor,
so that my heart was secretly enticed
and my hand offered them a kiss of homage,
then these also would be sins to be judged,
for I would have been unfaithful to God on high.
If I have rejoiced at my enemy's misfortune
    or gloated over the trouble that came to him –
I have not allowed my mouth to sin
    by invoking a curse against his life –
if the men of my household have never said,
    'Who has not had his fill of Job's meat?'–
but no stranger had to spend the night in the street,
    for my door was always open to the traveler –
if I have concealed my sin as men do,
    by hiding my guilt in my heart
because I so feared the crowd
    and so dreaded the contempt of the clans
    that I kept silent and would not go outside
(Oh, that I had someone to hear me!
I sign now my defense – let the Almighty answer me,
    let my accuser put his indictment in writing.
Surely, I would wear it on my shoulder,
    I would put it on like a crown.
I would give him an account of my every step,
    like a prince, I would approach him.) –
    if my land cries out against me
    and all its furrows are wet with tears,
if I have devoured its yield without payment
    or broken the spirit of its tenants,
then let briers come up instead of wheat
    and weeds instead of barley.' (Job 31:1-40)

THE HOLY SPIRIT DESCRIBES

As Job steps out from behind the speaker's platform, he hears hurtful slanderous words from those in the audience such as, "Lair. Unclean. Pervert. Sinner. Dirty old man!"

Job leaves the speaker's podium suffering shame and disgrace and returns to his law firm's backroom and lays down and falls into a deep sleep.

ADAPTED FROM THE UNABRIDGED
www.amazon.com Books Love & War by Joe Ragland
www.raglandministries.org/loveandwarbook/
BOOK NINE – Chapter 8

Scene Forty-Nine

Attorney Job Has a Dream and Rescues a Shepherd Girl

THE HOLY SPIRIT DESCRIBES

Job again arises from sitting among the ashes being afflicted '*with painful sores from the soles of his feet to the top of his head*' (Job 2:7-8), walking back to his law firm hearing cursing and slanders against him along the way. He finally unlocks the law office door, returns to his bedroom, and pulls back a purple bedspread and stripping down to his underwear crawls between the sheets and falls into a deep sleep.

Then in Job's dream, he sees Heaven open (For a similar experience see Acts 10:1), and something like a pure marriage sheet falling to the Earth.

THE HOLY SPIRIT SINGS

Then he heard a voice singing, "Arise, Job, and immediately travel to the well you had built for the travelers coming from Lebanon. Take a pure white sheet and your heavy iron rod you made to drive off wolves. Take the camel you borrowed back to your client, friend who lives near the well on your land."

Job awakes and selects a new white linen sheet he had been saving for a special occasion and his iron rod and ties his client friend's camel to the back of his camel. Job heads towards Job's Well, he dug as a youth.

As Job was proceeding out of town, sixty-six hateful shirtless males were blocking the road saying, "Stop! Where do you think you are going snakeskin skeleton man? How were the prostitutes? They were seen coming out of your law office. Confess your sins you are lying leper, who has reached the end of his life and pay us sixty-six dollars, and we will let you past.

Job spoke, "Lord, please spare their lives as they do not know what they are doing. I am on Your assignment. Help me to break through this blockade."

Job started the lead camel traveling as fast as it could with the middle largest boys being pushed back by unseen angels. Job gallops through them with the youth continuing to accuse and mock him with perverse words. When Job was out of sight and hearing of his accusers, the angels of the Lord froze the evil shirtless males. As they were frozen, two she-bears (For a similar occurrence see 1 Kings 2:24.) came out of the nearby woods and mauled all sixty-six with each crying, bleeding, and screaming for their mother. Without exception with each bleeding from the crude claw rakes and teeth marks on their naked chest, they temporarily looked worse than Job.

Now Job's client has a daughter named Joyce, who looked more like a boy than a girl, as she was flat chested, dark sunspots on her face and hands, with short hair looking more like a boy than a girl. Joyce was a shepherdess (Rachel was a shepherdess, who watered her sheep, e.g., see Geneses 20:9), who wrote songs about God's ways and tended her father's sheep. This day Joyce had brought the sheep to Job's Well for watering. As she was pouring water into a watering trench, she was hit in the back of the head and knocked to the ground. Three men were standing over her, although they thought she was a boy, with the leader Homoper declaring,

"Lad, this is our well, and these are our sheep. Also, I am going to abuse you and then behead you, and bury your body in that sand dune. I had not had a male lusting in days. These two dirty rotten scoundrels with me like women. Ugh."

Homoper orders, "You grab the lad's arms as I get me some male loving."

The men grabbed each arm and turned their heads away so not to look at the homosexual act and ultimate murder by beheading. While Homoper was undressing, Joyce cried out to the Lord,

"Father God, don't let them take my virginity and life. Help me! If You were in trouble as I am in trouble, I would help You. In the Name of Your Coming Son, Jesus! Amen!"

Homoper had stripped himself naked and was straddled down between the kicking legs saying,

"You little . . . How dare you kick me?"

Homoper pulling up the robe screams. "Where is your tallywhacker? It fell off. No, you are a girl! Ugh!

Another one named Sedu yelled, "I see her hymen. Let me have me a virgin."

The evil men pull her tunic over her head, revealing a brown bra pressing her small breast to her chest. They ripped off her bra exposing small pointed breast with Sedu lusting licking his lips,

As Sedu got naked, he licked his lips saying, "Nice. I will take my time with you, my virgin. Wow! Who could have ever guessed you had such a womanly figure under that robe? This first penetration will sting a little bit. You are my sixth virgin I have raped. "

Job was coming over the hill just as Joyce screamed again *Father God, help me!*" The evil men slammed Joyce to the ground with her fainting.

Job quietly exited his camel just as Sedu widens Joyce's legs as he drew near her hymen to penetrate her. He was only six inches away when Job hit Sedu right in the mouth with his heavy iron rod. The violent blow knocks out all of his front teeth with his gushing blood from his mouth going all over the naked stomach and private area of Joyce.

Job then turned to naked Homoper coming toward him, with a small sword and Job knocked out all of his front teeth with blood and teeth going everywhere. Then Pervert swings at Job barely missing him with his dagger with Job swinging his heavy iron staff with all his might and striking him in the mouth also knocking out all of his front teeth. Homoper gushing blood grabs Joyce's tunic pressing it to his lips, running away in terror across a nearby sand dome out of sight. Pervert and Sedu picking up their robes pressing them to their mouths trying to halt the gushing blood also in terror run after Homoper over the sand dome. Teeth were on the ground all around Joyce, who was lying naked and still unconscious having fainted from fright.

Both camels had walked up with the tied camel licking Joyce on the face. Joyce as she woke up seeing all the blood all over every place. Job walking backward toward her with a white sheet held behind his back approaching her when she says, "Job is that you?"

"Yes, Joyce. The Lord used me to rescue you. Thank God, I was at the right place at the right time. None of that blood is yours!"

Job holds the sheet behind his back requesting, "Here wrap this large sheet around you several times, and mount your camel."

JOYCE: Joyce with tears rolling down her cheeks, dripping off her chin spoke with gratitude,

"Brother Job, thank you for saving me again! You saved me once when I was only ten years old from a poison snake, as it was about to strike me, by your stomping its head. Also, there was another time you saved my life - it is just a shadow, but I dreamed about it, and I believe it happened. Let us ride slowly so my sheep can follow me home. They know my voice, and they will follow us."

JOB: Job not looking at her, answers, "Joyce I remember that time I killed that poisonous snake by stomping its head at the picnic. I remember you as a skinny little girl coming with your dad to my law office on various legal matters, but I don't remember ever saving your life before."

JOYCE: "Precious Job, my hero! You saved me once before in the First Earth Age from being raped and murdered. Do you not remember? I was rescuing young girls from a life of prostitution in the temple of the false god Poseidon. I was caught, and three of Atlas II's henchmen were sent to murder me, and they wanted to rape me first. In trying to murder you, they got confused and turned and killed themselves with laser guns. Also, I was with you in Paradise helping you proofread and bring to completion "*The Rise and Fall of Atlantis*," written by King Atlas. I thanked you then, and I thank you now. How could I ever repay you? Look, there is my dad."

"Dad, Job saved me from being raped and murdered now this second time and by being bitten by a poisonous snake at a picnic as a little girl. Dad, please take care of the sheep and Hump. Let me go in and get all this dried blood off me. It is not my blood. Job knocked out the teeth of the three evil men that attacked me. It is almost time for dinner. Please invite Job to stay for dinner. How can I ever repay him? He is my hero and my best friend! Thank you, Job!"

JOB: Job still not turning his head to look at Joyce said, "Dearest Joyce you are most kindly welcome! Bless the Lord Jesus, who had me at the right place in His timing."

Job and Joel sat in rocking chairs enjoying each other's fellowship awaiting Joyce's return.

JOB: "It was the Lord Jesus who saved her! I am only His humble servant. He is to have all the glory! You should see all those teeth scattered on the ground looking like popcorn. The Lord's angel guided my iron rod as I swing it with all my might. It is written and sung,

JOB SINGS

'For You (God) struck all my enemies on the jaw;
You have broken the teeth of the wicked.'(Psalm 3:7)
'The Lord laughs at the wicked,
For He knows their day (of final judgment) *is coming.'*(Psalm 37:13)
'You will only observe with your eyes and
see the punishment (sentence) *of the wicked.'* (Psalm 91:10)
Let us give God all the glory!
Hallelujah!"

JOEL: "No, Job. I give God the glory for using His chosen vessel to save my daughter's life! You are the bravest lawyer of them all! Today a law book was no good, as the only law, these evil men understood was your very heavy iron rod aimed by a mighty man of God, knocking out their front teeth. We have an enemy in this world, *'who comes, to steal, kill, and destroy.'* (John 10:10)

If it were not for you, I would be weeping tears right planning for her burial. How can I ever thank God and you, His servant, enough for sparing my daughter? Thank you again and again!"

JOB: "You are my friend, and you are most kindly welcome."

JOEL: Job and Joel sat silent when Joel breaks the silence, "You know my wife had earlier died in a high hurdle horse race. I warned her that this kind of sport was very dangerous. I understand you warned Nissa not to do camel racing on that narrow ledge. I am sorrow about the death of Nissa. I know you miss her."

JOB: "I do so much. We had perfect chemistry; at least for my part. If you might know a widow not too old, please let me know. *'It is not good for man to be alone!'* (Genesis 2:18)

THE HOLY SPIRIT DESCRIBES

Joyce appeared dressed in a pure white high neck long sleeve robe going down to the ground. Her short hair is almost dry. Joyce smiles at Job not saying a word. They went into the dining room with Job sitting across from Joyce with Joel offering the blessing in song,

JOEL PRAYS IN SONG

"Father God, thank you for my dear friend Job, whom You have used now three times to spare my daughter's life. Lord, he is looking for an older widow, but not too old, for it is not good for man to live alone! Do for him above which he cannot even think or imagine. Bless him, our friend. Bless our meal and fellowship together. We humbly ask this in the name of Your Son, Jesus. Amen!

Joyce shyly tries not to appear to admire Job so much during the meal. Joyce's eyes are tearing up with her having to wipe them with the cloth napkin in her lap, which became soaked with her tears.

JOEL: At the conclusion of the meal, Joel announced. "It is going to take a little more time for the cooking of our dessert. Let us go out on the veranda and light our torches. We have a full moon rising this evening in a few minutes. God made the lesser light to rule the night. Our special night of celebrating Joyce being alive."

JOYCE: On the way to the veranda, Joyce respectfully whispered to her dad, "Could I talk to you privately a moment."

JOEL: "Job, please go up to the gazebo with the lighted torches up the hill. We will be up shortly."

Joel asked Joyce, "What is it?"

JOYCE: "Dad, I have a secret I have to share with you."

JOEL: "Can it wait?"

JOYCE: "No, dad. It is about Job. I have had a secret crush on him ever since he saved my life in Atlantis. He does not remember it, but I faintly do. I even loved him in Paradise, even though there we had no giving or receiving in marriage. Please do not give him to an older widow! It would break my heart! He is not too old for me. I know where he is going, and I want to go back with him to Paradise. I love him! I have dreamed of being married to him. I have romantic powerful chemistry toward him. Please, dad, acknowledge the Lord's perfect Will in this for love's sake!"

Joel and Joyce sat down as the servants brought up the deserts.

JOB: "This is one of the most delicious deserts I have ever had."

JOEL: "How would you like something even more delicious than this?"

JOB REPLIED: "I couldn't image what would taste better than this."

JOEL: Joel responded with a song,

'Taste and see that the Lord is good;
Blessed is the man who takes refuge in Him.'(
(Psalm 34:8)

"Joyce and I have spoken, and we have you a wife."

JOB: "Good. You know I will be thirty-five next month. Just look at these wrinkles around my eyes. I have lost so much weight from an infection on my skin. Who would want me?
Possibly some aging widow with poor eyesight? I would hope the widow is not too old as I might like to have children again."

JOEL: Joel smiles, "No, she is not too old."

JOB: "Who is she? Do I know her?"

JOEL: "Yes, you know her. Would you like to be introduced to her?"

[Job nods a yes.]

JOYCE: Joel looks at Joyce with Joyce softly replying, "Me! I know I am skinny, have these dark sun spots on my face and the back of hands, my hair is short, but my hips are widening as a mother hopefully to be soon, as I would love to have children. I am ready to give up my tomboy ways and let my hair grow and be a loving wife and mother! I have loved you and dreamed of being married to you."

JOB: "Joyce, I am old enough to be your dad, "How old are you, like fourteen?"

JOYCE: Joyce smiles, "I will be sixteen next month. Only nineteen years' difference. Do you realize when you are 140 I will be 121?
I would like to have ten children, seven boys, and three girls. How does that sound? Job, I have loved you since you first saved my life in Atlantis. I would not even be alive on the Earth if it were not for you. I need a husband, and you need a wife. I will love, trust and honor you, if you will have this girl with damaged skin who loves you.

I know a girl is not supposed to propose, but I do not want to miss this opportunity not only for this lifetime, but also throughout eternity as I always want to be near you. What do you say?

JOB: Job swallowing hard rises and then bows on his right knee before Joyce, "Would you have this scabbed old man as your husband? I will love you and cherish you now and in the coming New Earth (Revelation 21:1)!"

JOYCE: Joyce, bending down, taking Job by his scabbed hands helping him to his feet looking him in the eyes smiling, "I will marry you! You will not be sorry! Praise God! We will have all eternity to enjoy each other!

We could get married on my sixteenth birthday next month right here on our veranda standing in this gazebo. On my birthday, another full moon is scheduled, and this one is a super blood moon."

JOYCE SINGS

When I fall in love, it will be forever
Or I'll never fall in love!
When I give my heart, it will be completely
Or I'll never give my heart!
And the moment I can feel
That you feel that way too
Is when I fall in love with you.
(Adapted from When I Fall in Love
by Edward Heyman and Victor Young)

JOB: Job takes Joyce's sun damaged hand, kissing it, and sings,

JOB SINGING

"My darling, thank you for loving me!
'God has taken away my shame!'
(Genesis 30:23.)
'There is a time (season) *for every*
activity (includes romantic marriage)
under Heaven.
. . .There is a time to cry
And a time to laugh.
There is a a time to mourn and a time to dance.
. . . There is a time to hug . . .
. . . There is a time to love . . . (our time has come)

. . . Two are better than one . . .
. . . A cord of three strains (Joyce, JESUS, Job)
is hard to break.'
(Ecclesiastes 3:1, 4, 7, 8; 4:9, 12)

Darling, I am in love with you!

304

ADAPTED FROM THE UNABRIDGED
www.amazon.com Books Love & War by Joe Ragland
www.raglandministries.org/loveandwarbook/
BOOK NINE – Chapter 9

Scene Fifty

Job's Second Wedding

THE HOLY SPIRIT DESCRIBES

Torches are blazing with the veranda being beautifully decorated, as the full moon rises. Job looks thin, with his face sunken in, with scabs showing on the exposed parts of his body. Job is wearing a white suit, white shoes, and a white silk bow tie with majestic blue stars of David. Job waits under an ornate Chupah, "*symbolizing the new home of the couple when they become husband and wife.*"

Joyce on her sixteen birthday, having hopefully just turned from girlhood to womanhood, also looks thin with dark sun spots on her face and hands from prolonged thermal sun damage, with her covering her face and damaged complexion with a veil. As the full moon rises, the marriage ceremony begins.

HARPIST SINGS

Youth and romance are not a time of life, but
God, the matchmaker, bringing two together as one.
as a matter of His perfect will
a quality of a beautiful soul,
a time of brightness and vigor of the
emotions, and the bounce and freshness of
the deep springs within.

Youth and romance mean courage over
timidity of the appetite,
exploring and adventures over
the love of ease.

You two reach forth in the joyful now
and to the good things daily and throughout
Eternity coming your way as you love God, keep
His commandments, rejoice in Him,
And with enthusiasm of life, you serve Him.

The harpist plays, "*Here comes the bride*," singing as the bride appears,
'Faithfully guided, draw near to where the blessing of marital love awaits.
Triumphant courage, the reward of virtue,
joins you two in faith as the happiest of couples!
Champions of love and grace, progress!
Jewels of marital romance proceed!
Faithfully guided, draw near to the blessings of marital love.
Triumphant courage, love, purity, joins you in faith, hope,
and love as the happiest and joyous of couples.

THE HOLY SPIRIT DESCRIBES

Joyce walks in white with a train behind her taking Joel by the arm who joyfully gives away his only daughter to his best friend, Job.

The ceremony deleted the phrase, "Until death do we part" as they never intended to part throughout eternity. During the marriage ceremony, both Job's and Joyce's eyes were open, and they saw Jesus accepting the invitation in prayer to attend the wedding with the hills and the sky being filled with angels. The full moon turns red as blood as the preacher decrees, "I pronounce you husband and wife You may now kiss the bride!"

After Joyce's veil had been pulled back away from her face, she received her first kiss from a man, her husband. [At the very moment of the kiss, the blood moon was in total eclipse.]

JOB: Job feeling like smoke was coming out his ears as the harp music played said, "Maybe we can cut short the reception."

JOYCE: Joyce smiles, "Maybe darling, but you will be known as a man of patience throughout eternity."

JOB: Job laughing, "I can be patient if it doesn't take too long!" (Both laughing)

THE HOLY SPIRIT DESCRIBES

Following the reception, a white carriage being drawn by four white horses arrives. Several pick up Joyce's train as she is seated on the love seat in the back with Job sitting beside her. Joyce turns with a smile as Job gives her a second warm kiss on the lips. White corn is being thrown by everyone saying such things as, "Be fruitful and multiply. Have fun on the honeymoon. Job remember to come up for air! Happy day when Jesus took your shame away! Romance in marriage is God's idea!"

Joel had restored his dad's beautiful white mansion on a hill overlooking the crystal clear Jordan River, located adjacent to Job's land and Joel had offered it to Job to use as a honeymoon resort. Job and Joyce sit leg pressing against leg under the light of a golden harvest full moon as the carriage commences down a brightly lit road with Mt. Zion in the distance.

Going up a beautiful moonlit hill, Job and Joyce look at a big banner across the top of a pure white mansion, also as a surprise to his daughter,

ENJOY THIS WEDDING PRESENT!
I desire my grandchildren near! Love, Joel

Servants meeting the carriage collect Joyce's train with Job walking hand-in-hand with her to the door, where he picks Joyce up in his arms with servants picking up Joyce's train as they proceed through the open door with Job carrying Joyce across the threshold inquiring,

JOB: "Where is the Master Bedroom?"

JOYCE: Joyce says, "Upstairs. I will navigate." With the servants dropping Joyce wedding train as Joyce steps up on the third step she remarks, "Darling, I don't believe I can pull this train up the steps. Do you want the servants to carry it up to our bedroom?

JOB: Job orders the servants holding the end of the train, "To the kitchen. No one looking! We will see you sometimes tomorrow."

Job unzips the back of Joyce's wedding dress pulling each sleeve over the dark sunspots on her hands. Job lets the wedding dress, settle to the floor.

JOYCE: Joyce is giggling in a white bra and panties, as it was a warm night, holding her husband's right hand saying, "Come let me show you! I have a wedding present for you. Remember, you are to be known as a man of patience!" (Laughing)

JOB: "Where is the Master Bedroom?"

JOYCE: Joyce says, "Upstairs. I will navigate

Joyce at the top of the stairs says, "Close your eyes!" She leads him into the Master bedroom saying, "Now open your eyes."

Job smiles with joy as he sees a white round bed trimmed in gold. The round bed had an antique white curved headboard with blur Stars of David, with a matching bedspread, turned back revealing Star of David sheets and matching silk pillowcases., inviting a delightful soon grand entrance! Joyce hands Job a wrapped present with a white bow with Stars of David. "Open it, darling!"

JOB: Job replied as he admired Joyce's thin womanly legs and small pointed breast under her bra, "Can't it wait until the morning?"

JOYCE: "Patience! (Laughing) I have been waiting for this moment. Let me enjoy every moment of it. You will not be disappointed! I am so in love with you! Let me sing you a love song the Holy Spirit showed me would be written and sung,"

JOYCE SINGING

'So this is love, Mmmmm
So this is love
So this is what makes life divine
I'm all aglow, Mmmmmm
And now I know
The key to all Heaven is mine
My heart has wings, Mmmmmm
And I can fly
I'll touch ev'ry star in the sky
So this is the miracle that I've been dreaming of
Mmmmm
Mmmmm
So this is love!'
(*So this is Love* written by Mack David, Al Hoffman, and
Jerry Livingston and sung in the musical *Cinderella*.)

THE HOLY SPIRIT DESCRIBES

Job sat on the bed, tearing the paper off. It was the most beautiful and masculine pajamas he had ever seen. One long set for Winter and one short set for Summer. Joyce went to the closet, pulling out a soft, feminine sleeping robe, and holding up another baby doll white sleeping outfit for Job to preview.

Job swallows hard not knowing what to say, remembering Joyce's word, "*Patience!*"

JOYCE: "Now darling Job, we have two matching bathrooms. Now go and get a good shower and brush your teeth for a night of kissing. It is going to take me a little longer as I have been longing for this moment ever since you rescued me in Atlantis. It seemed an impossible dream, with Joyce again singing,

JOYCE SINGS

For nothing is impossible with God.'(Luke 1:37)
A dream is a wish your heart makes
When you're fast asleep
In dreams, you lose your heartaches
Whatever you wish for, you keep.
Have faith in your dreams and someday
Your rainbow will come smiling thru.

No matter how your heart is grieving
If you keep on believing
the dream you wish will come true!
(A Dream is a Wish Your Heart Makes, written by Mack David, Al Hoffman,
and Jerry Livingston and sung in the musical *Cinderella)*

Now patiently wait for me in our round marriage bed."

THE HOLY SPIRIT DESCRIBES

Job waits, and waits, and finally, Joyce emerges wearing her soft white sleeping robe with buttons up the front. Joyce walks over to the bed looking down at her husband as she bends over to kiss him on the lips and starting to unbutton his top running her fingers through the hair on his chest. Job running his hands through her slightly grown out hair, enjoying the perfume she was wearing, and trying to pull her into the bed.

JOYCE: "Darling let us kneel beside the bed and consecrate in prayer, with thanksgiving, our pure and lovely marriage bed and all we do, including our lovemaking for the glory of God!"

Kneeling with Job's right arm around Joyce's shoulder and holding her hands with his left hand, he prays in song,

JOB'S PRAYER SONG

"Father God, thank You for giving me, Joyce. I will cherish her and love her like Your Son loves the saints in the church, which He will purchase with His blood. Bless the children of this union. May they be godly and our sons and daughters be pure and holy! Yes, Lord, let our daughters be beautiful and have a meek and quiet spirit like Joyce. Bless this marriage for Your glory and honor. In Your Son, Jesus' name. Amen!"

JOYCE: Joyce affirms in faith, in a soft feminine voice, 'Amen,' smiles, kisses him again, making kiss number three. With them embracing each other, rolling on the floor with Joyce saying, "In the bed! I have a few buttons, and you have more buttons than I do. I have nothing on under this. Our honeymoon night is not the place for a bra or panties. When God presented Eve to Adam as his wife, they both were naked and unashamed." (Genesis 2:25)

THE HOLY SPIRIT DESCRIBES

Now back in the marriage bed each focused on undressing the other. Joyce already had all the buttons undone rubbing her hands through the hair on Job's chest. The full moon shining through the sliding glass door was pouring romantic golden moonbeams of blessings on the round marital bed.

JOB: Job finally finished the last button and pulled back the front of Joyce's gown revealing her small pointed breasts as he kissed each, taking them one at a time into his mouth saying, "All over a mouth full is a waste!" (Both laughing)

JOYCE: "I was a little concern as they are so small, but they soon will be full of milk."

JOB: Job romancing, "They are beautiful and just right for me. I like them just the way my God designed them. They so satisfy me."

JOYCE: Joyce having worked on the last button on Job's bottoms, reaching in whispering, "Just right. Holy unto the Lord ready to consumate our marriage. I am also ready. I have waited for this moment in marriage all my life."

JOB: Job's hand slides down as Joyce opens her legs in submission to him. Job in anticipation completes the opening in the front of Joyce's gown with his left hand as Joyce allows Job to pull the sleeves off her arms. Joyce raises up, and Job pulls the robe out from under her and throws it landing it on a nearby chair saying, "Three points!" Job gently rolls over on top of Joyce bracing his weight on his elbows whispering, "I do not want to hurt you!"

JOYCE: Joyce replies, "I was made for such a time as this with the husband I love! Our honeymoon union is the proper use of my womanly part designed for you in marriage by God. Enjoy my precious lover!"

JOB: Job pushes against the hymen, exhausted and speaks, "I cannot break through. Am I hurting you?"

JOYCE: Joyce encourages, "No! Do not be timid. Push like a man! This is God's design between a husband and wife."

JOYCE SINGS

"The two will become one flesh.
So they are no longer two, but one."
(Mark 10:8)

Darling, you can do all things through Christ who strengthens you. The joy of the Lord is your strength. Just lay on me a moment and kiss me with passion."

JOB: Job having a second wind pushes hard, feeling the hymen splitting as he enters deeper and deeper inside his virgin smiling, "I have reached the bottom, and you are so tight. That is all I have. You have taken it all."

JOYCE: Joyce replies, "A perfect fit! I will always be your warm and loving virgin."

THE HOLY SPIRIT DESCRIBES

Job stays deep inside Joyce without moving for several minutes. Then, barely moving Job spurts deep inside Joyce, turning her over on her side out of a puddle of blood and staying inside her as they each go to sleep. As the dawn light awakens Job, with his now small penis still partly inside Joyce starting to grow hard and erect again, with Job making small moves trying not to wake Joyce when he hears her gentle feminine voice whispering,

JOYCE: "What a man God gave me. What a way to be awakened! We will have to do this often." (Shortly they both simultaneously climaxed together.)

While Job is relaxing and smiling, Joyce arises saying, "Do not be concerned about the sheets as I have a white rubber cover under them, and we have plenty of fresh round soft sheets. Do me a favor, strip off the sheets, and put them out the bedroom door into the hall. Here is a wet cloth to cleanse any leaked through blood on the white rubber mattress cover. It will quickly dry in the air. Wow! That was so refreshing and satisfying! Marriage is the great invention of God. One loving husband and one loving wife. I am thankful to God that I didn't miss such a blessing!"

As the bathroom door closes, Job looks at all the blood on the sheets singing for joy,

JOB SINGS A PRAYER

"Lord bless my precious virgin who saved herself for me! She is a perfect fit. Help me not to look back, except for our times in Atlantis and Paradise, which are only shadows. Thank you that my mind today is again clear thinking. It has been dull for weeks. A lot of toxins must have been collected and stored in my semen. All that toxin is gone now, thanks to my loving wife. I feel like a young man again. My sunken eyes and dark circles are much less this morning. The pain from the ugly scabs is less. Thank you, Lord Jesus, for Your severe mercy to me for giving me a warm and romantic wife! For Your glory, please take away the unsightly dark sunspots from, Joyce's hands and face."

Job showers and applies olive oil to the dry scabs all over his body. He goes to his suitcase selecting comfortable, masculine clothes. He slightly trims his beard and walks out on the balcony looking at the magnificent view of Cannon Land.

JOB SINGS

"Surely this is God's country! *Jerusalem, the City of God. Zion, lovely Zion. Show me how You desire me legally to preserve this promised land for future generations and for 'the new Jerusalem, coming down out of Heaven from God, prepared as* (not the actual bride) *a bride beautifully dressed for her husband.'* (Revelation 21:2.) *Father, I ask this in Your Son's name. Amen!"*

JOB: Glowing like an angel Joyce walks barefoot out on the balcony in a modest white short sun dress and sits down on Job's lap, kissing him all over his face filled with scabs and then on the lips. Job reaches for a small pointed breast, saying, *'May your breasts satisfy me always,'* (Proverbs 5:19) and placing his other hand on her bare legs suggests, "Back to bed?"

JOYCE: Joyce smiles, "Patience! Let us go up to the gazebo for a garden breakfast, and we can pick up here in bed when we return! Let us give the maid time to collect our marriage bed sheets, replace with fresh sheets, and to prepare an omelet and fruit breakfast. Take your sandals off and walk barefoot with me in this soft holy grass prayer garden. I like your hairy chest and your beard. Masculine! You are such a lover and friend!"

JOB: Job smiling says, "Darling, Joyce, look at all this land as far as you can see we together own it for the glory of God. I was able to obtain clear title to my dad's land from my adopted brothers and sisters. In addition, I inherited an equally large land mass connecting my land to the North, and the land we are on will probably be yours as your dad is full of days, but let us ask the Lord to let him see his grandchildren.

What should we do with all this land? I could ask my friend, Enoch, so close to God, but I will ask you first as you are my helpmate."

JOYCE: Joyce respectfully replies, "Sweetheart, history often repeats itself. In Atlantis, you faced this same issue. God gave you wisdom, and He will give you wisdom now."

JOB: "Shadows. Help me as I cannot remember."

JOYCE: "My Love, you were the wisest and bravest lawyer of all in the First Earth Age, and you judiciously obtained and deeded all your wonderful land in Loveland to a tax-exempt nonprofit corporation you established. Legally, this drove that evil, King Atlas II crazier, if possible, as he could not raise the taxes out of sight on this tax-exempt land, meaning the government could not legally obtain the property through the taxing process.

Sweetheart, I was just about ready in Atlantis to hint somehow through a mutual friend I had a crush on you. It was more than a crush as it was love from afar, but I was only fifteen. Like now, I was flat-chested and skinny. I thought they had killed you. I cried, and I thought I lost my chance of making you love me. I mistakenly thought I had lost you forever. I cried and cried over you, my darling.

JOYCE SINGS

'Crying (struggling in an area) *may remain for a night,*
but rejoicing (God gives direction) *comes in the morning.'*
(Psalm 30:5)

However, when I arrived in Paradise, I rejoiced to learn that you were alive. I looked at my breast, and they were almost as flat as a boy's, giving just a hint I had been a female in Atlantis. I still loved you and when I found you I volunteer to help you polish on King Atlas' works ***The Rise and Fall of Atlantis.***

JOB: Job inquired, "Is King Atlas here? Why are you and I allowed to come back? Only shadows, but I seem to remember your smile and youthful laugh and the somewhat grumpy King Atlas."

JOYCE: "Darling, King Atlas died on Earth, and he is not legally allowed to come back to be born of a woman in a subsequent Earth Age. *'It is appointed unto men once to die, and after that* (death on Earth) *to face judgment.'* (Hebrews 9:27) We were allowed to come back to the surface of the Earth as we were rescued alive out of the First Earth Age without dying.

JOYCE SINGS

'For God will command His angels concerning you
to guard you in all your ways;
they will lift you up in their hands,
so that you will not strike your foot against a stone.
You will tread upon the lion and the cobra,
you trample the great lion and the serpent (devil).
'Because he loves Me,' says the Lord, *'I will answer him.*
I will protect him, for He acknowledges My name.
He will call upon Me, and I will answer him!
I will be with him in trouble,
I will deliver him and honor him.
With long life will I (God) satisfy him
and show him My salvation.'
(Psalm 91:11-16)

Laser shots were hitting all around you when you jumped alive into the entrance to the Abyss on top of the Great Pyramid. You were then, today, and forever, my hero!"

Job do you know who was behind afflicting you *'with painful sores from the sole of your feet to the top of your head'?* (Job 2:7)

JOB: Job replied, "God? *'The Lord gave, and the Lord has taken away!'* (Job 1:21)

JOYCE: "No! It was the devil who *'comes only to steal and kill and destroy.'* (John 10:10)

The devil had King Atlas over Atlantis murdered with a laser gun. You once mentioned in Atlantis, before your mysterious disappearance, that if we ever desired a revival to call upon your friend Melchizedek. After we had built an outdoor preaching arena on the tax-exempt land you donated we invited Melchizedek to hold us a revival, and He preached repentance, salvation through Father God's Son, Jesus, new birth, and how much God loves those made in His image.

JOYCE SINGS

'God is love!' This is how (Father) *God showed His love among us: He sent His one and only Son as an atoning sacrifice (to pay in full the debt due) for our sins.*

. . . No one has ever seen (Father) *God, but if we love each other, God lives in us and his love is made complete in us.*

. . . Whoever lives in love lives in God, and God in him. Love is made complete among us so we will have confidence (of our eternal salvation) on the day of judgment, because . . . we (born again believers) *are like Him.'* (1 John 4:8-12, 16-17)

'Love never fails!' (1 Corinthians 13:8)

Darling, God, did not murder your children, or steal your flocks and herds, or inflict you with these painful sores. (See Job 2:7) Father God is love and for legal reasons of His own, He allowed Satan in his rebellion to attempt to destroy you. It was Apollyon Lucifer, now called Satan, who had sought to make you curse God and die. God knew you would not do this, but you would come forth as pure gold as you love God so very much!

What a day to remember when I was among the vast audience in the Dinosaur Dome in Atlantis as Melchizedek preached a great revival message of the love of God with two-thirds responding and coming forward for salvation. I looked up, and Satan's chief harp leader was desperately trying to come, but Satan had locked the door to the harp room. Homosexuals turned loose of the hands they were holding and came forward and were gloriously saved.

I later learned in Paradise that Melchizedek was none other than the Son of God, Jesus. He explained that Satan wanted, and still wants, to murder God the Father, His Son, Jesus, the Holy Spirit, Michael and Gabriel, the angels, and all we who love God living on the planet Earth.

314

Just before Satan set off his ice bomb, which caused the ice age, all of us being a part of the Kingdom of God worshiping God and rejoicing in such a great salvation in this glorious revival service in the Dinosaurs Dome were rescued by God. We saved ones joined you and King Atlas in the heart of planet Earth in Paradise.

JOYCE SINGS

'*For God so greatly loved and dearly prized the world* (those made in His image) *that He gave His only-begotten Son* (Jesus, to die on the cross to fully pay the penalty for the sins of all who receive Him as Savior) *so that whoever believes in* (trusts, clings to, relies on) *Him shall not perish – come to destruction, be lost* (in Hell) – *but have eternal* (everlasting) *life.*' (John 3:16)

Atlantis then sank into the sea, but all your land, you preserved for the Lord, will be duplicated again when there will be no longer any sea on the New Earth. (Revelation 21:1) You will legally also protect this land here in the promised land of Zion and consecrate it to God perpetually. Acknowledge the Lord in this and all your ways and He will direct your path. (Proverbs 3:5-6)

JOB: Job responds, "What a wise helper the Lord preserved for me. Now let us walk barefoot up to the gazebo to enjoy our honeymoon first breakfast. Remember where we left off here. (Laughter). Our best friend, Jesus, our Savior, Lord, and King have given us both our marriage and this honeymoon to enjoy.

JOYCE: "Look how skinny my arms are, and my skin is so ruined by the hot sun out with the sheep. I am skin and bones, and my hair is cut off looking like a boy's hair. I am letting it grow. It will take a long time. You will have to help fatten me up as out on the pastures with my sheep I mainly ate herbs and berries."

THE HOLY SPIRIT DESCRIBES

JOB: Job in joyful tears, praises, and thanks God, kisses Joyce's bony hand. He exited the house, walking up to a gazebo praying in silence in his heart,

"*Father God, Joyce makes me feel so much like a man. It was Your grace and love that finally brought us together. She is Your best reward for me. I missed You for not first acknowledging You on my marrying Nissa. I still have a place in my heart of love for Nissa. Help me! It is not right to love two women at the same time. I repent! Forgive me and show me any truth, I need to know. I love You with all my heart, mind, soul, and strength! I acknowledge You in this marriage, and bless Joyce and us for Your glory. I give you all the glory. In Jesus' name. Amen!*"

Job in joyful tears, praises, and thank God as he kisses Joyce's bony hand. He exited the house, walking up to a gazebo praying in silence in his heart,

Job and Joyce pause at the first landing for a kiss, and walking through red rose petals covering the path up to the gazebo all the way to the top of the hill. Walking barefoot in the rose petals each step stirs up beautiful perfume aromas. No roses have ever had such a delightful smell as these red Zion beauties. When they entered the gazebo, Job asks,

JOB: "Why the third plate?"

JOYCE: Joyce smiles, "Jesus, the Son of God, is always our honored guest at every meal. Let us always set a plate for Him. '*For nothing is impossible with God*! (Luke 1:37) Jesus may be seated here, right now!"

Job and Joyce smell the delightful breakfast dishes under the covers with candles beneath, keeping the Cheesy grits and huge platters of omelets warm outlined with baskets of nuts and blueberries and various tasty treats. Job pulls out the chair first for Jesus and then for Joyce."

Job and Joyce being seated hold hands while Job prays in song,

JOB PRAYS IN SONG

"Father God, Your Son, Jesus, is always our honored and welcome guest at every meal. What a wife you gave me to think of such a thing as setting a plate for Jesus, our best friend, Savior, and Lord. Bless our first breakfast together and our honeymoon. Whatever life I have left, I give it to You! Receive it as a half shekel in Your pocket and spend it, however, You chose.

I wish I had not wasted so much of my life already. Lord, make us one and may our marriage bring you glory and honor. You did, above all, that I could think or imagine! Joyce has a precious and beautiful heart and is a perfect fit for me. Help Joyce to gain a little weight and take away the sun spots on her face and hands for these are the desires of her heart. May I truly love her just like You Jesus Christ will love all the Saints You shed Your blood to save! In Jesus' name. Amen!"

JOYCE: Joyce agrees, "Amen! So be it!"

They kiss as they agreed after each prayer blessing their meals together.

JOB: Job looks at Joyce, who is smiling from ear to ear, inquiring, "My love, why are you smiling so much? It's only 9:00 in the morning."

JOYCE: Joyce, further smiling whispers, "The honey barrel has just fallen over me as we have a Breakfast Guest! Our best Friend is here! Open his eyes, Lord Jesus."

JESUS: Jesus spoke, "Brother Job, I brought wedding presents from My Father, the Holy Spirit, and Myself."

Job and Joyce had both fallen to their knees worshiping and looking up seeing a huge monitor screen with Atlas, with many of their best friends from Atlantis gathered, in the shape of a cross, singing,

KING ATLAS AND THOSE IN PARADISE SINGING

"This is our marriage song of worship, romance, grace, and praise;
Our song is of thanksgiving and joy.
For you were chosen before the foundation of the world,
To bear much fruit advancing the Kingdom of God.
His banner over you is love!
You are closer and pure than two cuddling doves.
You are His, and He is yours showing previews of His (Jesus') promised bride.
You are crowned with love, joy, peace, and rest.
His grace guides you with the joy of the Lord Jesus on your face.
You two will run this glorious journey ahead with joy, never to end!
In ten thousand years, you will have just begun an eternity of love under His amazing grace."

JOB AND JOYCE: Tears filled Job's and Joyce's eyes as they both said together to King Atlas and those in Paradise, "We love all of you and miss you! We don't desire to see you soon as we are on our honeymoon (laughter as generally there is no giving or receiving sexually in marriage in Paradise) and we are learning more about the good work we are to accomplish in this Second Earth Age for the glory of God."

Atlas smiles holding up his bound book and turning it showing its title,

THE RISE AND FALL OF ATLANTIS
By
Atlas
Edited by Job and Joyce

JOYCE: Joyce speaks, "Just say edited by Job as I was only his help-er."

KING ATLAS: Atlas replied, "What I have written I have written! Joyce, you also worked so hard on it. I put your name on the cover. I had no idea you two would be one in marriage. Everyone here in Paradise has read our book, and it will be read and studied by many throughout Eternity.

Joyce, you added the polishing eloquent feminine touches making this work just right for the glory of God! I am autographing this copy as a wedding gift to you. 'To: Job & Joyce, With love from Paradise. Atlas.' (It suddenly appears on the breakfast table.)

317

Job and Joyce you two also worked with the newlyweds Luther and Ruth in Paradise on our collection of songs given to you by the Son of God, Jesus.   Everyone here in Paradise sings your songs and those over in Hell can faintly hear the joy of our glorious salvation and love for the Lord.   Luther and Ruth are our song leaders and have asked to meet the newlyweds and to sing together from the *Treasures of Hallelujah Songs*. (Two copies suddenly appear on the breakfast table).

SONG LEADER LUTHER: "Ruth has a request from the Lord for Joyce, but first let us sing a few of our songs and the first song Job in a dream you received the catchy tune, which was borrowed in a song off in the future known as "John Brown's Body" published in 1856 by William Steffer, containing the salvation words, "The stars above in Heaven now are looking kindly down. His soul (John Brown died for the cause of Jesus) goes marching on (throughout eternity). *My Eyes Have Seen the Glory*." This tune was popular in camp-meeting songs during the American Christian revival movement known as the Second Great Awakening.   When new Christian faith, hope, trusting the Lord (**Jesus was their Lord**) words were added to the tune "John Brown's Body" it became the most popular marching song of the Union Army with the outbreak of the Civil War in 1861. The Confederate Army had nothing to compare to this inspiring Christian faith, hope, and trusting in God marching song.   Here are some early Paradise verions,

Mine Eyes Have Seen the Glory
(Lyrics by Joe Ragland)

Mine eyes have seen the glory of the salvation of the Lord.
He is shifting chaff from the wheat, before His judgment seat.
He has loosed His offer of salvation and a terrible swift sword.
Being saved is a safe, loving, and joyful treat!

The lost will cry, 'Mountains fall on us,
and hide us from the wrath of the Lamb!'
Come just as you are, for there is room for one more.
God's love, grace, and truth abound!

I'm not ashamed of the Lamb of God,
who paid the penalty I owed for my sin.
I repented, and with my new birth, I am awed.
Come to Jesus and win?

Jesus died to make men holy,
saving all who believe.
Let me live to help Him set sinners free,
Now come to Jesus and receive!

My Hero, Son of God, born of woman,
has crushed the serpent's head!
From that defeated adversary we saved ones,
have nothing to fear or dread.

Gabriel will sound the trumpet's blast,
and the dead will rise first.
All saved will be caught up,
with those left behind gasping,
the saved to never hunger or thirst.

Glory, glory, hallelujah!
Glory, glory, hallelujah!
Glory, glory, hallelujah
His salvation is marching on!

HALLELUJAH, JESUS
(Lyrics by Joe Ragland)

My Shepherd supplies all I need,
Lord Jesus is His Name.
In pastures green, I rest and feed,
alongside a peaceful stream.

When I stray, He brings me back,
to His fold of born again ones.
Jesus leads me in righteous tracks
as an adopted daughter or son.

When I walk thru the threats of death,
His presence gives me protection.
His Shepherd's staff and comforting rod,
delivers me with no rejection.

He favors me in the sight of my foes.
He feeds me on a table spread,
My cup of blessings overflow.
He pours the oil of blessing on my head.

My Lord's provisions and love follow me,
all my abundant life days.
His eternal house will be my glee,
with Hallelujah, Jesus I pray!

He brings me to a glorious place,
with Jesus on the throne.
I am not a stranger, nor a guest,
but a child safe at home.

RUTH: "Joyce may I place twelve more copies of *Treasures of Hallelujah Songs* in the transporter for you? The Lord Jesus requests that you, with the book of *Job*, place a few of these to be included in Noah's ark. The Book of Job will be included as part of the Bible to show the people of the world the way of salvation. Later a copy of our *Treasures of Hallelujah Songs* is to be given to man named Abram (later changed to Abraham), with a copy to be delivered to someone watching his father's sheep, a lad named David, the Son of Jesse. *Treasures of Hallelujah Songs* will assist David, who will become King of Israel, in his praise and worship to write a portion of Psalms, to be sung by the people who love God.

LUTHER: Let us conclude our portion by singing

Hallelujah! It is good to sing praises to our God. (Psalm 147:1)

I sing to the Lord (Jesus) because He has dealt bountifully with me. (Psalm 13:6)

My merry, happy, and joyful heart is like good medicine (brings healing). (Proverbs 17:22)

I sing and make music in my heart to the Lord. (Ephesian 5:19)

[Hallelujah means, "Praise the Lord". Psalms 146-150 all begins and ends with Hallelujah.]

JOB: "Joyce and I thank you for our signed copy of the historic *The Rise and Fall of Atlantis* and ministering together these faith building songs we previously sang in Paradise. . It was an honor working with all of you as *'the end of a matter is better than its beginning.'* (Ecclesiastes 7:8) King Atlas you have done it God's way this time!" (All from Atlantis viewing in Paradise laugh.)

KING ATLAS: King Atlas, who often hurtfully speaks the first thoughts coming into his mind, avers, "Joyce, how did you get so skinny. Your skin is so dark and spotted as if it has been baked and 'darkened by the sun.' What happened to your beautiful hair?"

JOYCE: Joyce laughs, "I didn't know a romantic man of God was coming my way. I was not thinking of myself as a female — more like a unisex. (Laughter) I was out in the sun all day tending my sheep acting like a tomboy. *'My own vineyard* (complexion) *I have neglected.'* (Song of Solomon 1:6b)

If I had known marital love would blow my way I would have taken better care of my skin and eaten a little better. I got so thin that the wind could almost blow me away. I apologize to all of you and especially to my husband for looking so ragged."

320

KING ATLAS: Atlas further spoke, "Job, you look like you have aged. You also look ragged. How did you get all those lines around your eyes and those scabs on your face and hands? You were always so youthful looking. You cannot be as old as you look."

JESUS: Jesus interrupts, "Atlas, silent! I desire all you dearly loved Saints in Atlantis to pray and now raise your right hand of blessings toward Job and Joyce on the screen. They have had to endure things up here on the surface of the Earth, but all of you know that I have a great work for them to complete here in this Second Earth Age. Remember how Job gathered all that land in Loveland, Atlantis for a non-profit tax-exempt organization to worship and serve Me, which legally kept your evil son from taxing the Atlantis Saints out of the place they own! Again, Heaven is in need of an anointed and faithful lawyer here to legally accomplish the same thing in the land of Zion!"

"Likewise, after the Earth is to be destroyed by water in this Second Earth Age, My friend, Abraham, in the Third Earth Age will be given all of Job's land deeds known as the Land of Cannon. Because of Job's legal work, I can legally promise Abraham, '*To your offspring* (seed) *I will give this land.*' (Genesis 12:7)

Adam legally gave the *rulership* of this world I gave him over to Satan when he obeyed Satan by choosing of his own '*free will*,' to knowingly disobey My one commandment to him! I mean what I command, and command what I mean to be obeyed!

Job will legally perfect legal title to certain key parcels of land. I will set up My earthly Kingdom right here in Jerusalem for a 1,000 years (Revelation 20:1-4) [A 1,000 years on Earth is like one day in Heaven. 2 Peter 3:8] at the conclusion of the Third Earth Age. My Father does all things legal, and nothing illegal, so obtaining perpetual title to this land legally is important.

Atlas, all of you in Paradise witness my wedding present to these two precious saints now one flesh. I warn you all not to speak any negative words over My anointed and blessed servant, Job!

Job you and Joyce stand up and receive your wedding present. Turn and look each other in the eyes.

Now I decree a special blessing on Job and Joyce now being one – spirit, soul, and body!

THE HOLY SPIRIT DESCRIBES

Immediately the aging and lines on Job's face and all scabs and skin defects disappear. Under his beard, he becomes fourteen years younger, with manhood muscles developing and again having a full head of hair.

Likewise, Joyce's dark spots on her skin disappeared with her complexion becoming glorious. Her skinny 87 lbs. frame now weighs 107 lbs., and her short hair grows halfway down her back. Joyce instantly becomes the most beautiful woman in all the land! Like mother, like daughters, as it will be written and sung,

THE SPIRIT OF JESUS SINGS

'*Nowhere in all the land were there found women as beautiful as Job's daughters.*'
(Job 42:15)

JOB: Job looks at Joyce and praising Jesus saying, "She always has been this lovely inside – wow – one would have to be a true man to fully appreciate Joyce's outward and inward beauty. Thank You, Lord Jesus, for blessing Joyce '*exceeding above all that we could ask or think.*' (Ephesians 3:20)

Lord Jesus, may Your bride likewise be even above all You, Son of God, can think or image, if that is possible. Jesus, we desire to be invited to the wedding banquet of the Lamb, who will die on a cross to pay the penalty our sins deserve.

Thank you for such a delightful and youthful wedding present. We as a couple will also give You the fruit of our marriage as our gift back to You and a special wedding present with others for you and your bride."

JESUS: "You two will be a future special blessing indeed! Joyce is a shadow and great-grandmother of My pure bride, and you will be given an honored place at the marriage banquet of the Lamb. Joyce, I have another assignment for you. I desire you to edit the first book of the Old Testament Covenant to be entitled "*Job*," ending with these words,

'*After this, Job lived a hundred and forty years. The Lord blessed the latter part of Job's life more than the first. He had fourteen thousand sheep, six thousand camels, a thousand yoke of oxen and a thousand donkeys. And he also had seven sons and three daughters. The first daughter he named Jemimah, the second Keziah and the third Keren-Happuch. Nowhere in all the land was there found women as beautiful as Job's daughters, and their father granted them an inheritance along with their brothers.*

After this, Job lived a hundred and forty years; he saw his children and their children to the fourth generation. And so he died, old and full of years.' (Job 42:12-36)

322

Jesus continued giving directions to Joyce, "Joyce, you will finish the book of *Job*, and your beautiful great granddaughter will marry **Shem** (Genesis 7;13) and personally take seven copies of the book of *Job* on the ark with Noah, and this will be a part of the *Bible* in the Third Earth Age. Joyce, you will live seventy days longer than your husband Job, and then you will die in such peace full of years, and you will join Job, and King Atlas in Paradise when you die full of years,

JESUS SINGS

'Precious in the sight of the Lord is the death of His faithful servants.'
(Psalm 116:15)

Job, on Earth with much joy, you and Joyce will have seven sons and three daughters. Joyce, you will first have twins - a boy and girl - one year from now. You will have another set of twins, and then you will have triplets. You two represent the righteous line of Abel, and I decree Joyce you will have little birth discomfort. You truly will be *'a joyful mother of children.'* (Psalm 113:9) It will be written and sung about a virtuous woman such as you,

JESUS SINGS

'A wife of noble character who can find?
She is worth far more than rubies.
Her husband has full confidence in her and lacks nothing of value.
She brings him good, not harm, all the days of her life.
She selects wool and flax and works with eager hands.
She is like the merchant ships, bringing her food from afar.
She gets up while it is still dark; she provides food for her family and
    portions for her servant girls.
She considers a field and buys it; out of her earnings, she plants a vineyard.
She sets about her work vigorously, her arms are strong for her tasks.
She sees that her trading is profitable, and her lamp does not go out at night.
    In her hand, she holds the distaff and grasps the spindle with her fingers.
She opens her arms to the poor and extends her hands to the needy.
When it snows, she has no fear for her household, for all of them are clothed in scarlet.
She makes coverings for her bed; she is clothed in fine linen and purple.
Her husband is respected at the city gate, where he takes his seat among the
    Elders of the land.
She makes linen garments and sells them, and supplies the merchants with sashes.
She is clothed with strength and dignity; she can laugh at the days to come.
She speaks with wisdom,   and faithful instruction is on her tongue.
She watches over the affairs of her household and does not eat the bread of idleness.

Her children arise and call her blessed; her husband also, and he praises her:
Many women do noble things, but you surpass them all.
Charm is deceptive, and beauty is fleeting, but a woman who fears the Lord is to be praised.
Give her the reward she has earned, and let her works bring her praise at the city gate.'

(Proverbs 31:10-31)

JESUS: Jesus further instructs, "I like and have chosen Job and Joyce! I desire you to encourage them in their writing of their work, ***Righteousness and Wickedness in the Second Earth Age – From Adam to Noah.*** The Holy Spirit will join My Spirit to the egg of a virgin woman to be born a baby having flesh, bone, and blood in the Third Earth Age. Like you Job I will pass the test and receive My pure bride. Blessings on you, Atlas and all those in Paradise, as Job and Joyce, are on their honeymoon.

They are my ideal beautiful holy and romantic married couple. Until we all meet again, Shalom Y'all! Job and Joyce let nothing move you. *Always give yourselves fully to the work of the Lord, because you know that your labor in the Lord is not in vain*! (See 1 Corinthians 15:58)

PARADISE SINGS A CLOSING SONG TO JOB AND JOYCE

"Love endures with patience *and* serenity, love is kind *and* thoughtful, and is not jealous *or* envious; love does not brag and is not proud *or* arrogant. [5]

It is not rude; it is not self-seeking, it is not provoked (nor overly sensitive and easily angered]),Love does not take into account a wrong *endured.*

It does not rejoice at injustice, but rejoices with the truth (when right and truth prevail).

Love bears all things [regardless of what comes], believes all things [looking for the best in each one], hopes all things [remaining steadfast during difficult times], endures all things (without weakening).

Love never fails [it never fades nor ends]. But as for prophecies, they will pass away; as for tongues, they will cease; as for the gift of special knowledge, it will pass away.

"(1 Corinthians 13:4-8)

The Screen in Paradise Goes Off

ADAPTED FROM THE UNABRIDGED
www.amazon.com Books Love & War by Joe Ragland
www.raglandministries.org/loveandwarbook/
BOOK NINE – Chapter 10

Scene Fifty-One

THE HOLY SPIRIT DESCRIBES

Attorney Job Vindicated by God and Finalizes Title Deeds to the Promised Land

Job Walks With Jesus

JOB: Seven days into the honeymoon Job whispers to Joyce, "I am going to go up to the gazebo and pray. I will be back in time for dinner."

Job prays and sings,

JOB SINGS IN PRAYER

"Father, I am looking back even in lovemaking to my love for Nissa. It is not good to love two women at the same time this much. Help me to become a one-woman man. In Jesus' name. Amen!"

JESUS: Jesus walks beside Job and in love explains, "You need to know some *'truth, which will set you free'* (John 8:32) in this area of your soul. Nissa and Lesba conspired to seduce you into marriage so they could have your land, making Nissa the largest landowner in the world. Whitestone and others warned you not to marry Nissa. She seduced you and tricked you into marrying her. Not all that glimmers is gold! She was Lesba's virgin, and they would lay out naked often on the roof having many sex toys as they brought each other to sexual climax. You ignored Whitestone's foundational teaching,

'Trust in the Lord with all your heart and lean not on your own understanding; in all your ways acknowledge Him, and He will make your paths straight.' Proverbs 3:5-6)

When you entered a marriage covenant with her, it was until death do you part. She wanted children to help with all aspects of the wine production, and to party with her and Lesba. She aborted eleven other of your children without telling you. I consider such a late-term abortion murder. She prided herself on being bisexual as she enjoyed sex with females and males. However, once someone enters a marriage covenant any other sexual activity with the same sex, the opposite sex, through the eyes, minds, or thoughts I consider adultery.

325

Remember back now on My law written on the Great Pyramid in Atlantis, reading in part,

THE SPIRIT OF TRUTH SINGS

The Ten Commandments
VI Thou shalt not kill
VII Thou shalt not commit adultery

All eleven of your aborted children have been taken to Paradise and taught the glorious things of God. Yes, you had twenty-one children with Nissa. She kept you entirely in the dark regarding the eleven she aborted helped by Lesba, who was an accessory to murder. Each of your aborted children has been told only that their mother murdered them without your knowledge and that their mother who did not care for them was also planning to murder their dad.

Each of your aborted children has read with delight *The Rise and Fall of Atlantis* and about their hero dad. Job, My friend, you are also a hero in My eyes, a mighty man of God, and in the eyes of all those in Paradise. I am mindful of all your labor and braveness in the Kingdom of God.

Yes, you missed Me on marrying Nissa. Repent and from now on first acknowledge Me in all your ways and lean not on your own understanding, and I will direct your paths.

We need this day to bring closure to Nissa as she was not truthful or faithful to you."

JOB: "What about the seven sons and three daughters that Nissa allowed to be born?"

JESUS: Jesus with tears in His eyes responds, "My Word is 'forever settled in Heaven' (Psalm 119:89), as it is written and sung,

THE SPIRIT OF TRUTH SINGS

"They exchanged the glory of God who lives forever for the worship of idols (here the moon and sex outside of marriage). Because they (each had a 'free will' habitually practicing and practicing the pleasures of such sins until their hearts were hardened feeling no guilt) did these things, God allowed them to pursue shameful passion. Women stopped desiring natural intimacy with a husband and started having unnatural lust with other women. In the same way, men stopped having natural relations with a wife. Men did shameful things with other men and were inflamed in their lust for each other. They brag about themselves (boastful). They invent ways to do evil. They do not obey their parents. They show no love or mercy to others."

(Romans 1:22-26, 30-32)

The evil companion Lesba corrupted your daughters mocking your repeated words to marry a believer in God. Your young daughters would lay upon the roof sunning naked with Lesba, who introduced them to drinking wine and to lewd lesbian acts. Two of your daughters had abortions from nights of wine drinking with unbelievers in God.

These aborted grandchildren are also in Paradise, and you can meet them later. Your sons were also corrupted and addicted to wine and homosexuality, and they aided, abetted, and were accessory to several abortions and the stealing of numerous vineyards, especially from widows and orphans.

I heard your prayers (Job 1:4-5) for your children, but prayer cannot overrule a human free will. I am a good God, and I know what I am doing. You warned your children often with tears, and their blood is not on your hands. Of their own 'free will,' they rejected Me as their Savior from sin and chose *'to enjoy the fleeting pleasures of sin for a season,'* (Hebrews 11:25) over such a great offer of eternal salvation. (See Hebrews 2:3)

Your wife, Nissa, and her lesbian lover, Lesba, were so evil they were planning on murdering you so Nissa would inherit your large tract of land to join with her land together making her the largest landowner in the world.

You remember that broken vial with a *'P'* on it lying beside Nissa's dead hand. Six drops of that in your food that evening would make you look like you had a heart attack. After you had refused her suggestions to curse Me and die, Lesba propositioned Nissa, 'Once Job is gone you will have all his land, and then we can get married as you are my virgin. You tricked him with that tomato juice on your bed sheet, but I saw the real blood when I pushed the ditto in you.

You admitted you like my loving better than Job's peanut. You could not stand the smell of Job's breath, and you stopped kissing him, but you never stopped kissing me. Same-sex marriages will be the marriages of the gods.'

When Lesba tossed the vial of poison to Nissa during the camel race, as Nissa was fumbling it with both hands, six (6) large King Cobras were sunning themselves in the middle of the trail just as they turned the bend. Lesba and Nissa were focusing on handing off the vial of poison not watching the mountain trail ahead. The King Cobra Vipers reared with hoods spread, showing long black tongues, preparing to strike at their camels' front legs, which caused the camels to stop suddenly throwing both Lesba and Nissa over their heads in the sharp curve with both screaming as they plunged to their death on the rocks and trees below.

You warned Nissa not to race, but she had no respect for your warnings or your words.

Because of Nissa's beauty, she thought she was it. You believed you had a good marriage because Nissa seemed warm to you in bed. Often during sex with you, Nissa would be thinking of climaxing with Lesba. She was Lesba's virgin, and Lesba had also stolen the virginity of your three daughters taking away their natural desire for husbands when they would all lay out naked sunning on the roof like snakes. Lesba introduced your sons to wine, homosexuality, and edged them on in stealing vineyards, especially those inherited by widows and orphans.

'This evil 'company corrupted good morals' (1 Corinthians 15:33) and destroyed the right and morals you sought to instill in your children.

Yes, the good you would seek to put into your children would be almost immediately stolen out of their hearts by the pleasures of sin. You rightly greatly feared that your children would reap destruction because of all their partying and choosing of their own 'free will' not to seek first the Kingdom of God.

You missed Me in this marriage by not first acknowledging Me, (Proverbs 3:5-6) as I would have directed your path away from Nissa. Now think of two secret passwords in your mind, without speaking them out, and when praying about a matter think those passwords (never speak them out as familiar evil spirits are watching) and you will hear in your born again spirit a 'yes' or a 'no.' I legally will not override a human's 'free will.' You of your own 'free will' gave Nissa your covenant, 'Until death, we do part.' I had to honor your marriage contract legally until death you did part! Now stop looking back as you parted! What does light have to do with darkness? Her ultimate end, with Satan, will be the lake of fire. (Revelation 20:15)

Now send someone old and trusted to confidentiality gather up for burning and burial all those lesbian evil tools hidden in the bottom drawer of the black cabinet up on the roof. Never go back to that evil place again. Board it up and let the sand of time cover it.

All Nissa's rights in that land, as you know being a lawyer, are now yours by operation of Zion law. I need you to do legally what you did with your land in Atlantis, as I have someone in the Third Earth Age, who will receive the deeds to this promised land. Yes, to Abram (Abraham) I will grant, 'All the land that you see I will (legally) give to you and your offspring forever,' (Genesis 13:15) which promised land I need for the Kingdom of God. I will set up an initial thousand-year reign (See Revelation 20:6) at the end of the Third Earth Age on this very land."

JOB: Job spoke, "May I see Nissa one last time in Hell?"

Jesus points and a monitor screen come down, zooming in on Hell itself.

JESUS: Jesus explains, "That is Nissa, who has managed with great effort to crawl out of the sea of liquid fire upon a rock.

Nissa is looking across a great gulf over to the other side, which from talking to those from the First Earth Age, she understands to be Paradise. All she can see of Paradise is a huge high overlook rock, which is called Glory Rock.

If Nissa listens carefully, she can faintly hear across the Great Gulf, children singing and playing, many of whom have been aborted or rescued right before the ice age explosion in Atlantis.

MAN IN HELL: One of the lost from Atlantis asks Nissa, "Why are you in Hell?"

NISSA: "Because I was planning on murdering my husband Job the very night I died when my camel threw me over its head."

MAN IN HELL: "I also was trying to murder in the First Earth Age with my laser gun a lawyer by the name of Job in Loveland, Atlantis. I do not see how I missed him, but all my shots struck all around him as if they were deflected. Just as I thought, I finally had a clear shot, lawyer Job jumped into a shaft known as the Abyss, which went down from the top of the Great Pyramid into this large place. Here we have a great gulf separating the two compartments — Paradise and Hell. Your husband in the Second Earth Age may have been the same lawyer?"

NISSA: "Describe Lawyer Job.

MAN IN HELL: "Attorney Job is skinny, having dark hair and skin, with strains of hair hanging down on each side of his head near his sideburns, with a hump on his nose, and he wore a red bow tie."

NISSA: "That's the same lawyer! I could not kill him either. It was like he had a hedge of protection around him."

"Point me to the top of the Abyss going up to the surface of the earth."

Nissa looked up and saw a constant fall of bodies counting them for a while. She responds, "I counted six hundred and sixty-six (666) fall in the middle of the Great Gulf, and be separated over into Hell. I only saw seven (7) fall in the midst of the Great Gulf be separated over into Paradise. One of those could have been Job as he looked near death when I last saw him. Is there a better place to look over into Paradise?"

"Yes, from Demon Rock you can see Glory Rock in Paradise."

"Show me!" [Swimming in a gulf of fire, they reach Demon Rock with a horrible looking demon grabbing the escort leaving Nissa digging with her fingernails into the rock and finally pulling her naked body up.]

LESBA: Lesba swimming by screams, "Nissa jerk me up out of these flames I am in such agony. There is a demon stalking me. Look how his claws have torn me across my chest. My flesh is hanging. I have been looking for you all over Hell. Are you hiding from me?

NISSA: Nissa, replied, "You are such a bitch! You got all my children and me in this horrible place of torment. Job warned me about this place and the necessity of staying pure and trusting in the Son of God for salvation, and repenting of my sins to avoid this horrible place."

Nissa pulls Lisba up saying, "You look terrible. Your flesh is hanging in shreds across your chest with no blood. What kind of body do we have here in Hell? Look at all those young girls falling into hell as they scream when they hit the flames with their clothes burning to ashes and becoming naked. Look at the ugly demon chasing after that one. He caught her as a crow on a roach. Look he is throwing her to another demon. You can tell from the girl' s face and long hair before she fell into the flames that she was a beauty on Earth. I wonder how she died?

The demons somehow get pleasure in hurting us. They seem to be only in partial torment, but their day is coming. Job warned me about, '*The lake of fire.*' (See Revelation 21:8) I tried to bite a demon that caught me, and it laughed and picked me up and threw me against a rock, and I could hear my bones breaking. Why did not somebody besides Job warn me of this horrible place? Why did not I believe Job? Why did not I listen to Job? Look, I see another one falling from the top of the Abyss and drifting over into Paradise, who is skinny and wearing something around his neck. He looks a little like my husband Job."

LESBA: On the screen were flames of fire with many screaming in agony in the flames. Lesba on Demon Rock asked Nissa, "What are you doing?"

NISSA: Nissa responds, "I am looking across that great gulf to that rock jutting out from Paradise hoping my husband Job might appear looking for me."

LESBA: "I was your real lover. You hated Job's breath and compared to what I used he was like a peanut. You loved me! You admitted that you married him for his land. We were planning on murdering Job for his land. We would have poisoned him, but for those nasty snakes. You would not have shed one tear for him or missed him in the least. We would still be wallowing in all that wealth if we could have murdered Job as planned.

You don't think he knows by now that you hated him and you were committing adultery with me on the side?"

NISSA: "Job is stupid when it comes to sex. One quickie at night and Job rolls over and sleeps like a baby refreshed to help others in law the next day. Stupid! I deceived and seduced him from the beginning. Land! Land! Land! That stupid jerk got all my land and property! I faked it. He was a peanut. The kiss on our wedding day was the last one I gave him, and I endured that one. I pretended my partial virginity, which I had given to you, with ketchup on the sheets as you suggested.

I hated Job. He helped others all the time - law, law, law! I hate to see him have all my land. With sex, I could turn Job whichever way I wanted. I had him hooked like a fish. My mother and grandmother did the same thing to their husbands. They taught me well to be a great pretender! If he appears on Glory Rock, I could talk him into getting me out of this place. After all, I am still his wife!"

JOB: A big split screen appears on Glory Rock for Nissa to view and hear as Job weeping brings closure, "Nissa, I just heard your testimony. You did deceive me. Our marriage was until death do us part. You failed in killing me and reaped death yourself. I warned you and our children with tears not to end up in this horrible Hell. Your blood is not on my hands. I warned you repeatedly. I will never come and speak to you again. Never! Don't look for me here, ever again. The answer is 'no' I cannot and will not help you get out of Hell.

'*It is appointed unto men* (and women) *to die once and after this the judgment.*' (Hebrews 9:27) Nissa, you had a human will, and instead of choosing the straight and narrow way of holiness you chose of your own '*free will*' the broad road of wickedness. I am asking Jesus to wipe away the tears from my eyes for you, for our children, and to take away my remembrance of your reaping destruction in Hell.

God gave you a '*free will.*' All you had to do in your life on the surface of the Earth was to receive Jesus, the Son of God, as your Savior, repent of your sins, and confess Jesus is your Lord. No one can tell how soon he or she may be at the gates of death. All people who reject God's free gift of His only begotten Son shall be turned into Hell. Perishing in Hell is the end of a Christless life. I will not be seeing or talking to you or our children ever again."

NISSA: Nissa responds, "Darling, you need a companion. A bed partner. I can keep you warm at night. You need a wife."

331

JOB: Job replied, "I have remarried. The Shepherdess you remarked once that had ruined her complexion out in the sun."

NISSA: Nissan mocked, "You could not have done worse! A flat chested tomboy, not a feminine bone in her skinny body. How could you be so stupid as to marry something like that? Be like two bones rubbing together."

JOB: Job responds to Nissa, "Joyce, and I have a blood covenant. She is my pure virgin. You ended our marriage. It is as if it had never been! I will remember you no more. Do not look or call for me again.
I am gone out of your existence forever – forever! You are on your own, without a husband's covering. You wanted it that way, and you have it. Bye forever!" [The screen goes blank.]

JESUS: Jesus comforts, "Job, you now *'know the truth, and the truth has set you free.'* (John 8:32) Job, I *'wipe away all your tears'* (Revelation 21:4) you might have for Nissa in this Second Earth Age. She premeditated and purposed in her heart to murder you. You are commanded to cast down any further thoughts of her after this day of truth!"

NISSA: In Hell, Nissa turns to Lesba and curses her, "You bitch, leave me alone! Hopeless! No hope of ever getting out of this horrible place. Because of you, I have no lawyer to present my case. No advocate to help get me out of here. If I ever see your wicked face, I will urge torture by six demons of you. I may be gaining favor with the master here!"
With that, a wave of flames sucked them both back into the sulfur burning lake with two horrible looking demons chasing each in different directions seeking to torment them further.

JOB: Job confessed, "Jesus, I have sinned against You! What should I do?"

JESUS: "You did not acknowledge Me and disobeyed me publicly. You need to humble yourself and repent publicly bowing down wearing under your robe sackcloth and pour ashes on your head after I question and admonish you openly. I will question you out of a storm in three Sabbath's from now in front of your accusers. Tell all the others that God will speak and that they are all invited as witnesses."

THE HOLY SPIRIT DESCRIBES

JOB INVITES HIS ACCUSERS TO A MEETING INDICATING THAT THE LORD WILL SPEAK THE TRUTH OUT OF A STORM

Job sets himself again before his accusers with Elihu having skill as a prosecuting attorney looking up at the darkening clouds, seeing the lightning storm overhead, and hearing the thunder continuing the accusations and condemnation against Job:

ELIHU'S ACCUSATION SONG

'*Listen*! *Listen to the roar of His voice,*
to the rumbling that comes from His mouth.
He unleashes His lightning beneath the whole heaven
and sends it to the ends of the Earth.
After that comes the sound of His roar!
He thunders with His majestic voice.
When His voice resounds,
He holds nothing back.
God's voice thunders in marvelous ways;
He does great things beyond our understanding.
. . .Listen to this, Job;
stop and consider God's wonders.
Do you know how God controls the clouds
and makes his lightning flash?
Do you know how the clouds hang poised,
those wonders of Him who has perfect knowledge?
. . .Tell us what we should say to Him;
we cannot draw up our case (like a lawyer) *because of our darkness.*
Should He be told that I want to speak?
Would any man ask to be swallowed up?
Now no one can look at the sun,
bright as it is in the skies
after the wind has swept them, clean.
Out of the north, He comes in golden splendor!
God comes in awesome majesty.
The Almighty is beyond our reach and exalted in power;
in His justice and great righteousness, He never punishes unfairly.'
(Job 37:2-5, 14-16, 19-20-23)

THE HOLY SPIRIT DESCRIBES

The sky grows darker still. Job removes his outer robe with sackcloth underneath, and he bows pouring ashes all over his head, in the deepest humility ever seen on Earth with tears of repentance flowing from his eyes. Then the Lord (Jesus) spoke to Job out of the storm,

JESUS SINGS

'Brace yourself like a man;
*   I will question you, and you shall answer me.*
Where were you when I laid the Earth's foundation?
*   Tell me, if you understand.*
Who marked off its dimensions? Surely, you know!
Who stretched a measuring line across it?
On what were its footings set,
*   or who laid its cornerstone -*
*   while the morning stars sang together*
and all the angels shouted for joy?

Who shut up the sea behind doors
*   when it burst forth from the womb,*
*   when I made the clouds its garment*
*   and wrapped it in thick darkness,*
*   when I fixed limits for it*
*   and set its doors and bars in place,*
*   when I said, 'This far you may come and no farther;*
*   here is where your proud waves halt'?*

Have you ever given orders to the morning,
*   or shown the dawn its place,*
*   that it might take the Earth by the edges*
*   and shake the wicked out of it?*
The Earth takes shape like clay under a seal;
*   its features stand out like those of a garment.*
The wicked are denied their light,
*   and their upraised arm is broken.*

Have you journeyed to the springs of the sea
*   or walked in the recesses of the deep?*
Have the gates of death been shown to you?
*   Have you seen the gates of the deepest darkness?*
Have you comprehended the vast expanses of the Earth?
Tell me, if you know all this.
Do you (lawyer) *know the laws of the Heaven.'*
*   (Job 38:1, 3-18, 33)*

. . .The Lord further said and sang to Job:

"Will the one who contends with the Almighty correct Him?
Let him who accuses God answer Him!"
    (Job 40:2)

Then Job answered the Lord in song,

JOB SINGS

"I am unworthy - how can I reply to You?
    I put my hand over my mouth.
I spoke once, but I have no answer –
    twice, but I will say no more."
        (Job 40:4-5)

Then the Lord spoke and sang to Job out of the storm,

JESUS SINGS

"Brace yourself like a man;
I will question you,
and you shall answer me.

Would you (lawyer) discredit my justice?
    Would you condemn me to justify yourself?
Do you have an arm like God's,
    and can your voice thunder like His?
Then adorn yourself with glory and splendor,
    and clothe yourself in honor and majesty.
Unleash the fury of Your wrath,
    look at all who are proud and bring them low,
look at all who are proud and humble them,
    crush the wicked where they stand.
Bury them all in the dust together;
    shroud their faces in the grave.' (Job 40:1-14)

. . . Can you pull in Leviathan with a fishhook
    or tie down its tongue with a rope?
Can you put a cord through its nose
    or pierce its jaw with a hook?
Will it keep begging you for mercy?
    Will it speak to you with gentle words?
Will it make an agreement with you
    for you to take it as your slave for life?
Can you make a pet of it like a bird
    or put it on a leash for the young women in your house?
Will traders barter for it?
    Will they divide it up among the merchants?
Can you fill its hide with harpoons
    or its head with fishing spears?

If you lay a hand on him,
  you will remember the struggle and never do it again!
Any hope of subduing him is false;
  the mere sight of him is overpowering.
No one is fierce enough to rouse him.
    Who then is able to stand against Me?
Who has a claim against Me that I must pay?
Everything under heaven belongs to Me.

I will not fail to speak of Leviathan's limbs,
  his strength, and its graceful form.
Who can strip off his outer coat?
    Who would approach him with a bridle?
Who dares open the doors of his mouth,
  ringed about with fearsome teeth?
Its back has rows of shields
  tightly sealed together;
each is so close to the next
  that no air can pass between.
They are joined fast to one another;
  they cling together and cannot be parted.
His snorting throws out flashes of light;
  his eyes are like the rays of dawn.
Flames stream from his mouth;
  sparks of fire shoot out.
Smoke pours from his nostrils
  as from a boiling pot over burning reeds.
Its breath sets coals ablaze,
  and flames dart from his mouth.
Strength resides in its neck;
  dismay goes before him.
The folds of his flesh are tightly joined;
  they are firm and immovable.
His chest is hard as rock,
  hard as a lower millstone.
When he rises up, the mighty are terrified,
  they retreat before its thrashing.
The sword that reaches him has no effect,
  nor does the spear or the dart or the javelin.
Iron it treats like straw
  and bronze like rotten wood.
Arrows do not make it flee;
  sling stones are like chaff to him.
A club seems to him but a piece of straw;
  he laughs at the rattling of the lance.

His undersides are jagged potsherds,
  leaving a trail in the mud like a threshing-sledge.
He makes the depths churn like a boiling caldron
  and stirs up the sea like a pot of ointment.
He leaves a glistening wake behind him;
  one would think the deep had white hair.
Nothing on Earth is his equal –
  a creature without fear.
 He looks down on all that are haughty;
  he is king over all that are proud.' (Job 41:1-34)

336

Then Job (very familiar with the Leviathans from his prior days in Atlantis) replies and sings to the Lord,

JOB REPLIES IN SONG

"I know that You (Lord) can do all things;
no purpose of Yours can be thwarted.
You asked, 'Who is this that obscures My plans without knowledge?'
Surely, I spoke of things I did not understand,
things too wonderful for me to know.

You (Lord Jesus) said, 'Listen now, and I will speak;
I will question you,
and you (Job) shall answer Me.'
My (Job's) ears had heard of You
but now my eyes have seen You.
Therefore, I despise myself
. . . and repent in dust and ashes.' (Job 42:1-6)

JESUS: The Lord responds, "You alone, who have humbled yourself, are forgiven."

JOB: Job replied, "Lord Jesus, also please forgive my accusers as they did know not what they were doing!"

It to be further written and sung in the book of Job,

JESUS SINGS

'After the Lord (Jesus) had said these things to Job, he said to Eliphaz the Temanite, '*I am angry with you and your two friends because you have not spoken the truth about Me, as My servant Job has. So now take seven bulls and seven rams and go to My servant Job, and sacrifice* (to God) *a burnt offering for yourselves. My servant Job will pray for you, and I will accept his prayer and not deal with you according to your folly. You have not spoken the truth about Me, as my servant Job has.*" So Eliphaz the Temanite, Bildad the Shuhite, and Zophar the Naamathite did what the Lord told them; and the Lord accepted Job's prayer.

After Job had prayed for his friends, the Lord restored Job's fortunes and gave him twice as much as he had before. (Job 42:7-10)

THE SPIRIT OF TRUTH SINGS

'. . . *The Lord blessed the latter part of Job's life more than the former part. He had fourteen thousand sheep, six thousand camels, a thousand yoke of oxen and a thousand donkeys. And he also had seven sons and three daughters. The first daughter he named Jemimah, the second Keziah, and the third Keren-Happuch. Nowhere in all the land were there found women as beautiful as Job's daughters, and their father granted them an inheritance along with their brothers.*'(Job 42:12-15. This inheritance consisted of silver, gold, and cattle to graze on land he loaned to them. Job gave no title to any land, retaining same for the Kingdom of God, as Job had done in the First Earth Age on the Island of Atlantis.)

THE HOLY SPIRIT DESCRIBES

Job had taught his daughters and their daughters to the fourth generation the importance of keeping pure and being a virgin on their wedding day as he believed that one of his descendant daughters would be the mother of the Savior of the World, the second Adam, the Messiah, who would legally overcome and crush the devil's head. (See Genesis 3:15)

Job had earlier cursed the day of his birth, when he did not know it was Satan trying to destroy him, by decreeing, "*May the day of my birth perish, and the night it was said, 'A boy is born*!' (Job 3:3)

Therefore, the male line of Job would not be recorded by name. However, the Book of Job preserved for all eternity opens, '*Job was the greatest* (richest) *among all the people of the East.'* (Job 1:3)

Job was grieved as the enemy of God, the devil, was spreading great wickedness over the Earth seeking to corrupt everyone. God would need one virgin woman to give birth to a male child (Jesus) who would crush the devil's head. God showed Job in a dream that the Earth would be destroyed again, this time not by the devil in an ice age, but by God Himself in a great flood.

When Job was very old and full of many joyful years his great-granddaughter, Charity, married a carpenter's son, by the name of Noah, who was the son of Lamech, who was the son of Methuselah, who was the son of Enoch. (See Genesis 5:21-29) Job shared his dream with them about the great flood coming.

Job indicated to them, he had a treasure chest of gold, a treasure chest of silver, and a sealed clay pot containing all the deeds of the lands of Zion and these were to be given to a man God would designate and change his name from Abram to Abraham, meaning the father of nations. Also, Noah was to use funds from the treasure chest to buy the material to build the ark, to support himself and his family. Job entrusted these to Noah with a smile on his face kisses his great-granddaughter on the cheek and blesses her and Noah and their future family saying, "Keep good notes until you see the rainbow (See Genesis 3:13) as I am going to need you when you arrive in Paradise to help me finish, ***Righteousness and Wickedness in the Second Earth Age – From Adam to Noah***. After saying a joyful goodbye to Noah and his family, he had finished his life's work and could die with dignity as it would be written about him,

THE SPIRIT OF TRUTH SINGS

'*After this, Job lived a hundred and forty years; he saw his children and their children to the fourth generation. And so Job died, an old man and full of years.'* (Job 42:16)

THE HOLY SPIRIT DESCRIBES

The great-granddaughter of Job and Joyce, Charity, gave 10 copies of the *Treasurers of Hallelujah Songs* and seven copies of **The Book of Job** to Noah to carry in sealed pots on the ark.

The Book of Job would be a book followed by the songs of David in Psalm to be included in the Old Testament Bible to be used by the people of Zion in the Third Earth Age. The book of Job speaks of the Leviathan (Job 41:1; Job 40:15 speaks of the Behemoth.) so visible in the Atlantic Ocean in the First Earth Age.

ATTORNEY JOB RETURNS TO PARADISE

All Paradise rejoiced with the return of Job. Job never went near Glory Rock as he purposed in his heart to never encounter again his adulterous wife, Nissa.. Soon after Job's death, Joyce joined him bringing copies of *The Book of Job* she completed shortly after Job's death. Both received youthfulness and joyfully living together in the same mansion in Paradise. Job sings in Paradise with Joyce at his side,

JOB SINGS

I give You thanks forever, Lord Jesus, for showing me the truth.
Praise You for the love of a wife, and using her to encourage and respect me as a man.
You are the Divine Matchmaker for every man, who seeks first Your kingdom and righteousness.
Thank You for giving me wisdom, joy, and strength in loving and serving You.
For you made a wife for her husband to help, comfort, and encourage him. (1 Corinthians 11:9)
Jesus, you have flesh and bone, and when you become a
a man born of a woman, I wish You a similar pure bride who loves You.
Yes, it is not good for a man to be alone.
Our Father God invented marriage between one male and female.
Such pure romantic love never fails throughout eternity.
I will tell of all Your wonderful deeds and goodness and mercy showed me.
I will be glad and rejoice in You, my Savior and best friend.
I will sing the praises of Your name, O Most High.
I will give thanks to You throughout the eternities of eternity

Job and Joyce finished the work, *Righteousness and Wickedness in the Second Earth Age – From Adam to Noah* adding a closing part about the Great Flood, and the book of Job which was read throughout Paradise and preserved in the archives of Heaven as the Third Earth Age was about to begin. They so enjoyed leading the songs from the *The Treasures of Hallelujah* songs, and selected one to amplify and sing over those for war in Hell,

Hallelujah
(by Joe Ragland)

Now I've heard there was a Heaven above.
A secret place of safety and love.
But many don't care about and are ashamed of Jesus Christ, are you?
The beaten and crucified, King of Glory bids me come, the best thing I ever did (done)!
So I came in childlike faith and was surprised by joyfully being born again.
Instead of Hell, I awoke in the age of grace on my way to glorious Heaven.
'Hallelujah'

The Lover of your soul invites you to the wedding supper of the Lamb.
I have my invite, and I can save you a seat as the wedding hall will be quite full.
I understand there is room for more, for whosoever will may come.
But many don't really care for marital romance, what about you?
Do you have faith and a desire to receive such a great salvation?
I joyfully sing the King of Glory's Hallelujah wedding song, what about you?
'Hallelujah'

HALLELUJAH, JESUS
(By Joe Ragland)

My Shepherd supplies all I need,
Lord Jesus is His Name.
In pastures green, I rest and feed,
alongside a peaceful stream.

When I stray, He brings me back,
to His fold of born again ones.
Jesus leads me in righteous tracks
as an adopted daughter or son.

When I walk thru the threats of death,
His presence gives me protection.
His Shepherd's staff and comforting rod,
delivers me with no rejection.

He favors me in the sight of my foes.
He feeds me on a table spread,
My cup of blessings overflow.
He pours the oil of blessing on my head.

My Lord's provisions and love follow me,
all my abundant life days.
His eternal house will be my glee,
with Hallelujah, Jesus I pray!

He brings me to a glorious place,
with Jesus on the throne.
I am not a stranger, nor a guest,
but a child safe at home.

NISSA SCREAMS A NEW SONG FROM HELL OVER INTO PARADISE

NISSA: Nissa in Hell screams, "That is my husband in Paradise singing a war song against us. Let us sing the opposite against the enemy,
Hate, hate, defiance! Hate, hate, defiance! Hate, hate, defiance!

JOB'S CLOSING ARGUMENT SONG

But I will sing of God's strength,
in the morning I will sing of God's love;
for God is my Defender (refuge; fortress),
my place of safety in times of trouble.
God is my strength1 I sing praises (of Hallelujahs) to
the Father, the Son, and the Holy Spirit being one God.
God is my Defender (Advocate; fortress)!
For Jesus, God's Son loves (and has saved) me.
(Adapted from Psalm 59:16-17)
**Blessed are those invited, and choosing to attend
of their own 'free will,' the Marriage
Supper of the Lamb, Jesus, the Son of God!**
(Revelation 19:7)

ADAPTED FROM THE UNABRIDGED
www.amaxon.com Books Love & War by Joe Ragland'
www.raglandministries.org/loveandwarbook
BOOK TEN – Chapter 1

Scene Fifty-Two

Noah, Earth Destroyed by Water, and Third Earth Age Begins

THE HOLY SPIRIT DESCRIBES

Nissa Summoned before the Prince of Darkness

The hideous demons, Woe and Moe, locate Nissa, the former wife of Job, suffering in the flames of Hell and indicate to her that the Prince of Darkness wants an audience with her. She accompanies them to a stairway guarded by other demons that let them pass. She is met on the stairs by Nickelodeon, who was formerly a temple prostitute. She affirms to Nissa that the great Lucifer wants an audience with her.

NICKELODEON: Nickelodeon explained to Nissa, "The great proud, beautiful one might crave to make you one of his cats. I am his leopard cat. Here is a cheetah cat outfit you can put on since you cheated on Job. (Smirking) You are to bow down and worship Lucifer when you come into his presence. You are not to speak a word until you are first spoken to and asked a question by the master. It is better being up here than down in the flames. Here are a comb and some makeup powder. Even here, this is still a place with no water."

Nickelodeon escorts Nissa into the throne room of darkness. Lucifer dressed in black velour, looking like a Spanish prince, is seated on the throne. Nickelodeon and Nissa hit their knees worshiping Lucifer. Nickelodeon whispers to Nissa, "Have you ever seen anything so beautiful!"

NISSA: Nissa replied, "Never! He would take my breath away if I had any breath. (Both unable to even laugh.) It will be a privilege to serve him. Ever had a hug from him?" [Silence.]

SATAN: Lucifer growls, "Nissa, I understand you were married for a time to Attorney Job. I believe one of Job's great grandchildren will give birth to something seeking to crush my head. (Genesis 3:13) I am determined not to let this happen! What do you know about this prophecy? Tell me all you know!"

NISSA: "Master, whom I worship, I remember my husband Job talking about the Messiah to come. The battle is between light and darkness. Job explained that some men love darkness more than light because their deeds were evil.

In the tornado, you sent, you killed all the male and female children I bore Job. Job told me he had remarried so maybe he has a male child by his new wife."

The Devil Screams in Anger

SATAN: Lucifer, scolding in anger, "How could Job get a message to you in my kingdom? Someone told me about that monitor on Glory Rock looking over into Hell. That is illegal! Hell is my jurisdiction, and I control the airwaves and the sight-waves. If I appointed you as my Cheetah, selected by me like a queen of darkness, could you protect my beautiful head from being crushed? I liked your advancing that although we had lost the battle, we will win the war,

> Hate, hate, defiance!
> Hate, hate, defiance!
> Hate, hate, defiance!

I like this battle march chorus for the Army of Darkness. You will receive great rewards for serving me. What do you say, Nissa?"

NISSA: "Purr. Job always rubbed my Cheetah cat's fur the wrong way. I will help you trace Noah's DNA."

SATAN: Lucifer orders, "Cheetah, my reporting demons, familiar spirits, will now report directly to you. Your assignment is to kill or corrupt every one of Job's children and all in that pure, undefiled line from Seth. Nickelodeon escort Cheetah, formerly Nissa, to her desk in the black war room."

Humans Increasing on the Earth in Second Earth Age as Nissa Directs Corruption of Those in the World

THE SPIRIT OF TRUTH SINGS

'*When human beings began to increase in number on the Earth and daughters were born to them, the sons of God* (godly lineage - Adam-Seth, Kenan-Mahalalel-Jared-Enoch-Methuselah-Lamech grandsons*) saw that the daughters of humans were beautiful* (although from the ungodly lineage of Cain, who murdered Abel, given over to shameful sinful ways, and serving false gods), *and they* (godly men*) married any of them* (knowing better than to marry ungodly women) *they chose. Then the Lord said, 'My Spirit will not contend with humans forever, for they are mortal; their days will be* (cut back life on Earth) *a hundred and twenty years.*'

The Nephilim were on the earth in those days – and also afterward – when the sons of God went to the daughters of humans and had children by them who became men of a (great) name and were the mighty warriors of long ago.

The Lord saw how great the wickedness of the human race had become on the Earth, and that every inclination of the thoughts of the human heart was only evil all the time. The Lord regretted that he had made human beings on the earth, and his heart was deeply troubled.

So the Lord said, 'I will wipe from the face of the earth the human race I have created - and with them the animals, the birds and the creatures that move along the ground – for I regret I have made them.' But Noah found favor (grace) in the eyes of the Lord.' (Genesis 6:1-8)

SATAN: After some time, Satan in confusion calls in his war cabinet, inquiring, "Is Noah a son of Job? Cheetah, Nissa, answer me!"

NISSA: "No. Noah is not a son of Job. However, one of Job's great-granddaughters named Charity married Noah. We either have successfully polluted Job's grandsons with beautiful wicked wives, homosexuality, or have killed them all. I understood that the Messiah will come through the male line."

SATAN: Satan angrily responds, "You fool! The Messiah will be from a woman - the seed of a woman. My enemy decreed,

SATAN SINGS

'And I will put enmity between you and the woman, and between your offspring and hers. He will crush your head, and you will strike his heel.' (Genesis 3:15)

Nissa, I mean Cheetah, did you corrupt Job's three daughters?"

NISSA: "Master, we also have corrupted the pure bloodline of two of Job's three daughters. However, Job's youngest daughter, Keren-Happuch, great-granddaughter, Charity, married Noah, and she has borne Noah three sons - Shem, Ham, and Japheth. (See Genesis 6:10)

SATAN: Satan orders, "Now corrupt Noah's three sons!" Nissa, queen of darkness, what is the plan?"

NISSA: Nissa replied, "Alcohol and homosexuality to start! We are seeking to corrupt Noah's sons. We have one leaning toward homo-sexuality. Just need a little push like to his eye gate. The land is full of violence and lust for sex and power.

Crazy Noah is building a big boat in the middle of the desert far from any water. He is preaching repentance and offering salvation from a destructive flood to anyone who believes his message about the Son of God. We will watch him since he married one of Job's great-granddaughters."

THE SPIRIT OF TRUTH SINGS

'*Noah pleased and found grace* (favor) *in the eyes of the Lord.*'
(Genesis 6:8.)

Like Job, Noah was a just man who acknowledged the Lord in all his ways. The **Bible** records,

THE SPIRIT OF TRUTH SINGS

''*Noah was a righteous man, blameless among the people of his time, and he walked faithfully with God. Noah had three sons: Shem, Ham, and Japheth.*

Now the Earth was corrupt in God's sight and was full of violence. God saw how corrupt the earth had become, for all the people on earth had corrupted their ways. So God said to Noah, 'I am going to put an end to all people, for the Earth is filled with violence because of them. I am surely going to destroy both them and the Earth. So make yourself an ark of cypress wood; make rooms in it and coat it with pitch inside and out. This is how you are to build it: The ark is to be three hundred cubits long, fifty cubits wide, and thirty cubits high. Make a roof for it, leaving below the roof an opening one cubit high all around. Put a door on the side of the ark and make lower, middle, and upper decks. I am going to bring floodwaters on the Earth to destroy all life under the heavens, every creature that has the breath of life in it. Everything on Earth will perish. But I will establish my covenant (the Seed of the woman, the Messiah, would legally crush the head of God's enemy) *with you, and you will enter the ark – you and your sons and your wife and your sons' wives with you. You are to bring into the ark two of all living creatures, male and female, to keep them alive with you. Two of every kind of bird, of every kind of animal and of every kind of creature that moves along the ground will come to you to be kept alive. You are to take every kind of food to be eaten and store it away as food for you and for them.''*

Noah did everything just as God commanded him.'' (Genesis 6:9-22).

THE HOLY SPIRIT DESCRIBES

The local sexually immoral and evil people of the Earth called him – 'Crazy Noah' – and the sinful people '*mocked and spit on him*' (See Mark 10:34 as they likewise many did this to Jesus, the Son of God.) as he built a large boat out in the desert over a period of 120 years, inland not in sight of any body of water.

Noah's evil neighbors, who were enjoying the pleasures of all manner of sin, would come out, mock, and laughed at Noah and God. They saw no need to be rescued from God's judgment. They took no thought about God, their souls, or eternity. They did not believe Noah that a rainstorm was coming. They would look up laughing not seeing even a cloud in the sky.

344

THE SPIRIT OF TRUTH SINGS

'Noah was '*a preacher of righteousness.*'
(2 Peter 2:5)

[Noah obeyed God, continually preached to those mocking him, and Noah warned them.]

NOAH PREACHES IN SONG

"Repent and turn from your wicked ways, or you will die in your sins when the flood comes. The evil you are practicing has not escaped God's all-seeing eye! God bade me warn you that unless you repent you will '*die in your sin*' (See Ezekiel 33:9) and perish in Hell. I warn you of the impending judgment, and your blood is not on my hands!

Now accept the free gift of eternal life by repenting and receiving God's Son, Jesus, as your Savior. Confess Jesus before men as your Lord. Eternal life means abundant life with God the Father, God the Holy Spirit, and God the Son forever. A storm is coming to clean the Earth. Get on board with me and be rescued from the coming destruction."

MOCKERS SINGING

MOCKERS: "Noah, it's getting mighty dry. Did your God finally die?"

NOAH: "My great Father God is very much alive. Repent and receive Father God's Son, Jesus, as Savior and come aboard and you will not have to die. I found grace in the eyes of the Lord, and you can find grace and mercy and be saved from the great tribulation flood coming to purify the Earth."

MOCKERS: "Crazy skinny Noah, where did you find that pretty wife and such lovely wives for your attractive hunks of sons. Share them with us, and we will help you paint your boat on the side with these words 'Fool for God' on each side would be appropriate. "

THE HOLY SPIRIT DESCRIBES AND SINGS

Earth Destroyed by Flood

One day the judgment rains started, and as the waters rose, evil people pounded on the side of the ark screaming for Noah to let them in, but it was too late as God Himself had '*shut the door.*' (Genesis 7:16) The same floodwaters that brought judgment and destruction to so many brought safety to Noah and his family.

345

It would later be written in the **Bible** of the judgment-cleansing flood,

'. . . *On that very day Noah and his sons, Shem, Ham, and Japheth, together with his wife and the wives of his three sons, entered the ark. They had with them every wild animal according to its kind, all livestock according to their kinds, every creature that moves along the ground, according to its kind, and every bird according to its kind, everything with wings. Pairs of all creatures that have the breath of life in them came to Noah and entered the ark. The animals going in were male and female of every living thing, as God had commanded Noah. Then the Lord shut him in.*

For forty days, the flood kept coming on the Earth, and as the waters increased, they lifted the ark high above the earth. The waters rose and increased greatly on the earth, and the ark floated on the surface of the water. They rose greatly on the Earth, and all the high mountains under the entire heavens were covered. The waters rose and covered the mountains to a depth of more than fifteen cubits. Every living thing that moved on land perished – birds, livestock, wild animals, all the creatures that swarm over the earth, and all mankind. Everything on dry land that had the breath of life in its nostrils died. Every living thing on the face of the Earth was wiped out; people and animals and the creatures that move along the ground and the birds were wiped from the Earth. Only Noah was left and those with him in the ark.'

(Genesis 7:13-23)

Third Earth Age Begins with Rainbow Covenant
THE HOLY SPIRIT DESCRIBES AND SINGS

'. . . At the end of the hundred and fifty days the water had gone down, and on the seventeenth day of the seventh month, the ark came to rest on the mountain of Ararat. Then God said to Noah, 'Come out of the ark, you and your wife and your sons and their wives. Bring out every kind of living creature with you – the birds, the animals, and all the creatures that move along the ground – so they can multiply on the Earth and be fruitful and increase in number on it.'

So Noah came out, with his sons and his wife and his sons' wives. All the animals and all the creatures that move along the ground and all the birds – everything that moves on land – came out of the ark, one kind after another.

Then Noah built an altar to the Lord, and, taking some of all the clean animals and clean birds, he sacrificed burnt offerings on it. The Lord smelled the pleasing aroma and said in His heart: 'Never again will I curse the ground because of humans, even though every inclination of the human heart is evil from childhood. And never again will I destroy all living creatures by water.'

'*As long as the* (First) *Earth continues, planting and harvest, cold and heat, summer and winter, day and night will not stop.'* (Genesis 8:2, 15-22)

'. . . *Then God said to Noah and to his sons with him: 'I now establish My covenant with you and with your descendants after you and with every living creature with you – the birds, the livestock, and all the wild animals, all those that came out of the ark with you – every living creature on Earth.*

I establish my covenant with you: Never again will all life be destroyed by the waters of a flood; never again will there be a flood to destroy the Earth.'

346

And God said, 'This is the sign of the covenant I am making between Me and you and every living creature with you, a covenant for all generations to come: I have set my rainbow in the clouds, and it will be the sign of the covenant between Me and the Earth.

Whenever I bring clouds over the earth, and the rainbow appears in the clouds, I will remember my covenant between Me and you and all living creatures of every kind. Never again will the waters become a flood to destroy all life. Whenever the rainbow appears in the clouds, I will see it and remember the everlasting covenant between God and all living creatures of every kind on the earth.'

So God said to Noah, 'This is the sign of the covenant I have established between Me and all life on the Earth.' (Genesis 9:8-17)

It is further written regarding the homosexual act of one of Noah's sons, Ham,

'Noah, a man of the soil, proceeded to plant a vineyard. When he drank some of its wine, he became drunk and lay uncovered inside his tent. Ham, the father of Canaan, saw (gazed with lustful gratification) *his father naked and told* (with sensual delight) *his two brothers outside. But Shem and Japheth took a garment and laid it across their shoulders, and then they walked in backward* (grieved at the suggestion of an opportunity of homosexuality) *and covered their father's naked body. Their faces were turned the other way so they would not see their father naked.*

When Noah awoke from his wine and found out what his youngest son had done (outraged at the homosexual lust) *to him, he said,*

'Cursed (because of homosexual impurity) be Canaan! The lowest of slaves will he be to his brothers.'

He also said, 'Praise (promised Seed of a woman, the Messiah, to legally crush the head of God's enemy is coming) *be to the Lord, the God of Shem! May Canaan be the slave of Shem. May God extend Japheth's territory; may Japheth live in the tents of Shem, and may Canaan* (lascivious homosexuality) *be the slave of Japheth.'* (Genesis 9:20-27)

Earth Land Divided – Europe and Africa from North and South America

'Sons were also born to Shem, whose older brother was Japheth; Shem was the ancestor of all the sons of Eber.

. . . Two sons were born to Eber: One was named Peleg, because in his time **the Earth** (Europe and Africa from North and South America) ***was divided*** *. . .* (Genesis 10:21-25)

. . . When Peleg had lived 30 years, he became the father of Reu. And after he became the father of Reu, Peleg lived 209 years and had other sons and daughters.

When Reu had lived 32 years, he became the father of Serug. And after he became the father of Serug, Reu lived 207 years and had other sons and daughters.

When Serug had lived 30 years, he became the father of Nahor. And after he became the father of Nahor, Serug lived 200 years and had other sons and daughters. When Nahor had lived 29 years, he became the father of Terah.

And after he became the father of Terah, Nahor lived 119 years and had other sons and daughters. After Terah had lived 70 years, he became the father of Abram (later named changed to Abraham), *Nahor and Haran.'* (Genesis 11:18-26)

It is further written in the Bible regarding Abram,

'The Lord had said to Abram, 'Go from your country, your people, and your father's house-hold to the land I will show you. I will make you into a great nation, and I will bless you. I will make your name great, and you will be a blessing. I will bless those who bless you, and whoever curses you I will curse, and all peoples on Earth will be blessed through you.'

So Abram went, as the Lord had told him, and Lot went with him. Abram was seventy-five years old when he set out from Harran. He took his wife Sarai, his nephew Lot, all the posses-sions they had accumulated and the people they had acquired in Harran, and they set out for the land of Canaan, and they arrived there.

Abram traveled through the land as far as the site of the great tree of Moreh at Shechem. At that time, the Canaanites were in the land. The Lord appeared to Abram and said, 'To your off-spring I will give this land.' (Genesis 12:1-7)

THE HOLY SPIRIT DESCRIBES

Abram Given Deeds Prepared by Job to Land of Canaan, Including Sodom and Gomorrah

MELCHIZEDEK: Melchizedek, being the Son and God, Jesus, later met and gave to Abram a sealed jar containing the deeds to all the gathered land in Zion prepared, by Attorney Job in the Second Earth Age, saying, "Go and record all these deeds in the land records!

Abram, let me ask you a question: 'Was Noah a success?'"

ABRAM: Abram smiles, "I guess so, or I would not be here in the Third Earth Age!"

MELCHIZEDEK: Melchizedek replied, "Yes, and from your seed the Messiah, who will crush the devil's head, will be born in this Third Earth Age."

THE HOLY SPIRIT DESCRIBES

Noah preached for a hundred and twenty (120) years and trusted God without one convert. The Son of God will preach three years and also be mocked and spit upon. It will be written,

'Jesus testifies to what He has seen and heard, but no one accepts His testimony (evidence as being true).' (John 3:32)

'From this time many of His disciples turned back and no longer followed Him (Jesus).

'You do not want to leave too, do you?' Jesus asked the Twelve.

Simon Peter answered Him, 'Lord, to whom shall we go? You have the words of eternal life. We believe and know You are the Holy One (Messiah) *of God.'* (John 6:66-69)

'His (Jesus) *appearance* (in being beaten and crucified to shed His life's blood on a cross) *was so disfigured He did not look like a man; His form so changed they could barely tell He was human.'* (Isaiah 52:14)

Noah was a great success as he kept the bloodline pure down to King David, and ultimately down to a young girl, who without the sperm of a man, gave virgin birth to the Messiah. Jesus, the Messiah, crushed the devil's head by shedding His life's blood, dying on a cross and being resurrected from the dead. Noah trusted in God to deliver him, and Jesus trusted in His Father God to raise Him from the dead.

The resurrected Messiah will decree,

'All authority in Heaven and on Earth has been given to Me. Therefore, go and make disciples (those who accept Jesus as Savior and confess Him as their Lord) *of all nations, baptizing them in the name of the Father and of the Son and of the Holy Spirit, and teaching them to obey everything I* (Jesus) *have commanded you. And surely I* (Jesus) *will be with you always, to the very end of the age* (first Earth passes away with a New Earth ahead for the born again saints).' (Matthew 28:18-20; See Revelation 20:15, 21:21)

It will be written describing the end of this Third Earth Age,

'. . . Because of the increase of wickedness, the love of most will grow cold, but he who stands firm to the end will be saved. And this gospel of the kingdom will be preached in the whole world as a testimony to all nations, and then the end will come.

. . . For then there will be great distress, unequaled from the beginning of the world until now - and never to be equaled again. If those days had not been cut short, no one would survive, but for the sake of the elect (born again ones), *those days will be shortened.*

. . . Heaven and Earth will pass away, but my words will never pass away.

No one knows about that day or hour, not even the angels in heaven, nor the Son, but only the Father. As it was in the days of Noah, so it will be at the coming of the Son of Man. For in the days before the flood, people were eating and drinking, marrying and giving in marriage, up to the day Noah entered the ark; and they knew nothing about what would happen until the flood came and took them all away. That is how it will be at the coming of the Son of Man (at the end of the age).' (Matthew 24:12-14, 21-22, 29, 35-39)

'By faith Noah, when warned about things not yet seen, in holy fear built an ark to save his family. By his faith, he condemned the world and became heir of the righteousness that comes by faith.' (Matthew 24:12-14, 21-22, 29, 35-39)

'For Christ died for sins once for all, the righteous for the unrighteous, to bring you to God. He was put to death in the body but made alive by the (Holy) *Spirit, through whom also, He went and preached to the spirits in prison* (those in Hell beneath the surface of the Earth) *who disobeyed long ago when God waited patiently in the days of Noah while the ark was being built. In it only a few people, eight in all were saved . . . .'* (1 Peter 3:18-20)

'For if God did not spare angels when they sinned, but sent them to Hell, putting them in gloomy dungeons to be held for judgment, if He did not spare the ancient world when He brought the flood on its ungodly people, but protected Noah, a preacher of righteousness, and seven others . . . (and) *if this is so, then the Lord knows how to rescue godly men from trials and to hold the unrighteous* (wicked ones) *for the day of judgment, while continuing their punishment.'* (2 Peter 4-5, 9)

Noah: An Example of a Righteous Man of Faith

'By faith Noah, when he was warned about things not yet seen, in holy fear built an ark to save his family. By his faith, he condemned the world and became heir of the righteousness that comes by faith.' (Hebrews 11:8)

ADAPTED FROM THE UNABRIDGED
www.amaxon.com Books Love & War by Joe Ragland'
www.raglandministries.org/loveandwarbook
BOOK TEN – Chapter 2

Scene Fifty-Three

King Saul in Hell

FATHER: **The Father says to Jesus**, His Son, and the Holy Spirit, "Let us watch as Nissa interviews King Saul in Hell as she seeks to destroy King David and his pure seed line from which You, My Son will be born of a virgin :

Nissa Interviews King Saul in Hell

NISSA: Nissa cross-examines, "King Saul, I brought you in to give you a little relief from the flames. I am Nissa, Job's first wife on Earth, and our master needs your assistance in developing a plan to destroy your enemy King David. He stole your crown! You had the right to remain king. Thank you for choosing to join us!

KING SAUL: "Queen Nissa, I never intended to come here. I had justified matters otherwise in my mind. I thought my scheme to get rid of my enemy David would succeed. When David was dead, I would just tell God that I was sorrow and ask Him to forgive me. Death came to me unexpectedly as a thief. Death outwitted me. Death was too quick for me. I stupidly thought I had plenty of time. Oh, my cursed foolishness! I was prideful in flattering myself, building my kingdom with vain dreams, believing I would live forever and be king forever. I was just saying peace and safety, and then sudden destruction came upon me. It was like labor pain on a pregnant woman. (See 1 Thessalonians 5:3.) It wasn't my fault, you know?"

NISSA: "King Saul you committed suicide, self-murder, by falling on your sword!"

KING SAUL: "Do you get all here who commit suicide?

NISSA: "No, not all, but most. Some are not in their right mind and go to Paradise. Let us cut out the small talk. Give me a key on how to destroy David! If our Goliath couldn't kill him, how can he be destroyed?"

KING SAUL: Saul presents, "I was going to die from the battle wound I had received. If I had not committed suicide, my enemies would have captured me, put my eyes out, and paraded me for all to mock. What happened to my physical body on Earth after I murdered myself?"

NISSA: "What happened to your physical body is not important to our discussion today! I desire your counsel on how we can finally destroy King David!"

KING SAUL: King Saul thinks, '*Oh, that someone would give me a drink of water from the well near the gate in Bethlehem.*' (2 Samuel 23:15) Nissa, I know the answer to your questions, but I will not tell you the answer until you tell me what happened to my body and where is my son Jonathan? May I see him?"

NISSA: "Yes, he is right across the great gulf over in Paradise. Several have seen relatives from Glory Rock. So tell me how we can destroy King David, and I will take you to Glory Rock to see your son!"

KING SAUL: "Not until you tell me what happened to my body!"

NISSA: "It would be best if you didn't know!"

KING SAUL: "Nissa, I am concluding the conversation!"

NISSA: "Okay, I have a copy of a scroll entitled '*Saul Takes His Life*' in my fire proof file folder and let me read it, 'Now the Philistines fought against Israel; the Israelites fled before them, and many fell dead on Mount Gilboa. The Philistines were in hot pursuit of Saul and his sons, and they killed his sons Jonathan, Abinadab, and Malki-Shua. The fighting grew fierce around Saul, and when the archers overtook him, they wounded him critically. Saul said to his armor-bearer, "Draw your sword and run me through, or these uncircumcised fellows will come and run me through, and abuse me." But his armor-bearer was terrified and would not do it; so Saul took his sword and fell on it. When the armor-bearer saw that Saul was dead, he too fell on his sword and died with him. So Saul and his three sons and his armor-bearer and all his men died together that same day. When the Israelites along the valley and those across the Jordan saw that the Israelite army had fled and that Saul and his sons had died, they abandoned their towns and fled. And the Philistines came and occupied them.

351

The next day, when the Philistines came to strip the dead, they found Saul and his three sons fallen on Mount Gilboa. They cut off Saul's head and stripped off his armor, and they sent messengers throughout the land of the Philistines to proclaim the news in the temple of their idols and among their people. They put his armor in the temple of the Ashtoreths and fastened his body to the wall of Beth Shan. When the people of Jabesh Gilead heard what the Philistines had done to Saul, all their valiant men marched through the night to Beth Shan. They took down the bodies of Saul and his sons from the wall of Beth Shan and went to Jabesh, where they burned them. Then they took their bones and buried them under a tamarisk tree at Jabesh, and they fasted seven days.' (1 Samuel 31:1-13)

KING SAUL: Saul argues, "Well, I shouldn't have been transported to Hell by your demons for killing myself like this. God is unjust to permit you to grab me."

NISSA: Nissa speaks sarcastically, "Just because you consulted with a witch, disobeyed God's command by not killing a captured king and his pregnant queen, with her escaping, keeping your enemy's cattle instead of killing them as commanded and murdering yourself all was no big deal! You had minor violations of God's commands. Now, how can we tempt King David to do worse than your little disobediences?"

KING SAUL: "Nissa, why do you want to destroy David? What is the big deal?"

NISSA: "That is of no interest to you! How can we defile (make unclean; corrupt) David? I did my part!"

KING SAUL: King Saul starts a multitude of words, saying, "Queen Nissa, David won my daughter as a prize when he killed Goliath. When I realized he was trying to steal my kingship, I gave her to another man. I then rightly sought to kill my competitor David.

Someone here in Hell told me that David thought he was a hot shot by illegally wearing a priestly garment, a linen ephod, and danced before the Lord with all his might. If one looked closely at times, his private parts were often exposed as he leaped in dancing. That rightly disgusted my daughter Michal, and she despised him in her heart. (2 Samuel 6:16) David has a real sex drive and knowing Micah, she has cut him off cold turkey.

Therefore, if you could tempt him to commit adultery and force him into murdering her husband, that ought to do it! That would top any wrongdoing I did!"

NISSA: "I like it! Guards take King Saul to Glory Rock and permit him to come back here only if I send for him."

Jonathan Counsels King Saul in Hell from Paradise

King Saul, dumped by Nissa's guards on Glory Rock, looks up into Paradise seeing his son Jonathan.

JONATHAN: Jonathan warns, "Dad give no information to God's enemy! Satan is a liar and a murderer. In your present hateful and appalling condition, you would be unhappy here in Paradise.

In Hell, they are for war, and you need not study war anymore. We are learning about walking in love for *'love endures all things and never fails.'* (1 Corinthians 13:5-6) After Hell and its final inhabitants are thrown into the Lake of Fire, (Revelations 20:14) it will be written and sung,

JONATHAN SINGS TO HIS DAD

'The Lord (Jesus, Son of God) *will teach us* (overcoming saints) *His way;*
so we may walk in His paths.
His instructions will go out from Jerusalem.
The Lord will settle disputes among many nations
They shall beat their swords (instruments of war) *into plow blades*
and their spears (instruments of war) *into hooks for pruning trees.*
Neither shall they learn (the ways of) *war anymore;*
but they shall all sit under their own vines
and under their own fig trees (symbols of prosperity),
and no one shall make them afraid.' (Micah 4:3-4)

Daddy, I made a covenant with David always to protect him as I love him as myself. (1 Samuel 1:18)

Do not touch God's anointed!' (Psalm 105:15)

You have sinned greatly, but nothing is impossible with God!

'Behold, I am the Lord, the God of all flesh. Is there anything too hard for Me?' (Jeremiah 32:27)

Dad, now repent on your knees in earnest with sincere humility! *'God is opposed to the proud, but gives grace unto the humble!'* (James 4:6) It is not over until it is over! That whole place you are in will be thrown into the lake of fire. (Revelation 20:14-15) The devil has declared war on God and His anointed ones, but he cannot win. His doom will be recorded.

JONATHAN SINGS

'The devil will go out to deceive the nations in the four corners of the earth – Gog and Magog – to gather them for battle. In number, they are like the sand on the seashore. They marched across the breadth of the Earth and surrounded the camp of God's people, the city (Jerusalem) *He loves. But fire came down from Heaven and devoured them. And the devil, who deceived them, was thrown into the lake of fire. . . Then I saw a great white throne and Him* (Jesus, Son of God) *who was seated on it. . . . I saw the dead, great and small, standing before the throne, and books were opened. Another book was opened, which is the book of life. The dead were judged according to what they had done as recorded in the books. The sea gave up the dead in it, and death and Hell gave up the dead in them, and each person was judged according to what he had done. Then Death and Hell were thrown into the lake of fire. The lake of fire is the second death. If anyone's name was not found written in the book of life, he was thrown into the lake of fire.'* (Revelation 20:7-15)

Dad, if you don't humble yourself, repent, trust in the blood of Jesus to cleanse you, receive Jesus as your Savior, and confess Jesus as your Lord, you will be doomed with the devil, and I can never see and enjoy you again. Now you practice walking in love even in Hell. You are a spirit in prison. God's Son will, take back what the devil stole from Adam. Adam and Eve are right here with me in joyful Paradise. They are forgiven, saved, and happy. He joked with me yesterday about never asking for his rib back. Adam repented, received his forgiveness, forgave himself, forgave others, and so can you!

Be prepared the best you can for that glorious day when Jesus will preach *'to the spirits in prison.'* (1 Peter 3:19) That will be your now opportunity day,

'For God says, 'In the time of My favor, I heard you, and in the day of salvation I helped you.' I tell you, **now** *is the time of God's favor,* **now** *is the day of salvation.'* (2 Corinthians 6:2)

Remember to be a man of few or no words! Like Job, be a man of patience, knowing that your *'Redeemer* (Jesus) *lives.'* (Job 19:25) After Jesus is crucified on a cross, shedding His life's blood to pay the penalty for sins of those who will receive Him as Savior, He will be grabbed by demons and thrown into Hell with you. Jesus will then preach here in Hades, comprising of two separated compartments Hell and Paradise. (See Matthew 12:40; Acts 2:27; Ephesians 4:8-9) Jesus will then take all the inhabitants of Paradise with Him up to Heaven."

'When He (the resurrected Jesus) *ascended on high* (back to Heaven),
He led captives . . . .
What does 'He ascended' mean except He also descended to the lower
Earthly regions (Hell and Paradise)*?'* (Ephesians 4:8-9)

354

KING SAUL: Saul naked in humiliation responds, "Jonathan, I receive your wise counsel. I am thankful to God for your giving me this secret hope of getting out of this horrible place, knowing that God's Son will in the fullness of time march into Hell for a Heavenly cause.

I plead Jesus' shed Blood! Satan, I renounce you and your demons. Jesus is my Lord. I repent of involvement with witchcraft, pride, idolatry, self-murder, jealousy, speaking curses over David, pride, and willful disobedience to God's commands.

I cup my hands and put all my shortcomings in them and cast all (1 Peter 5:7) up to God believing He still hears and cares for me. I ask You, Father God, to forgive me and give me another chance to be part of Your Kingdom under King Jesus. I believe the upcoming shed blood of Jesus will be poured out to pay the penalty my sins deserve. Satan, I renounce you, and I surrender my eternity to Jesus. Father God, led me, guide me, and give me the patience of Job, in the name of Your Son, Jesus. I receive by faith, even here in Hell, Your forgiveness. Since You have forgiven me, I now forgive myself! My past shortcomings are all behind me. I speak the protective blood of Jesus over me, and I plead the blood and name of Jesus to cover me even here in Hell. I am determined to walk in love as I sincerely repent and stand on the Scripture, *"Love never fails!"* (1 Corinthians 13:8) By the blood and name of Jesus, I proclaim,'*Though my sins are like scarlet, they shall be as white as snow, though they are red as crimson, they shall be like* (the whitest) *wool.*' (Isaiah 1:18) I thank You, Father God, for Your mercy and forgiveness! Shalom! In Jesus' name and by His blood. Amen!

JONATHAN: Jonathan in faith responds, "Amen! So be it! Shalom! Be patient and give no more aid to God's enemy! Be prepared for Jesus' appearance to run to Him falling at His feet, pleading His shed blood, and walk in love even in Hell. Dad, I love you!"

KING SAUL IN HELL SINGS SOFTLY IN PRAYER

Dear Father in Heaven,
I repent of giving aid to the enemy and for disobeying You.
You were right in allowing my sins to send me to this horrible place.
I repent and am so sorry for my sins against You and Your anointed, David.
Wash away my sins and guilt in the name of Your Son, Jesus, who I believe
will pay the penalty I owe for my sins, by being nailed to a cross, in my place, and
for all who will believe and confess Jesus as Savior and Lord.
Jesus, when you '*preach to the spirits in prison*' (1 Peter 3:19) receive and rescue me.
Create in me a clean heart and grant me the joy of Your salvation!
Let me go with You, Jesus, to Paradise, and I will praise and worship
God forever for being merciful and gracious to this one who died in sin.
By faith, I receive Your forgiveness and anointing even in Hell.
In Jesus' name, Amen!

355

ADAPTED FROM THE UNABRIDGED
www.amaxon.com Books Love & War by Joe Ragland'
www.raglandministries.org/loveandwarbook
BOOK TEN – Chapter 3

Scene Fifty-Four

Hell's Plan to Defile King David's Pure Bloodline

THE SPIRIT OF TRUTH SINGS

'I am God, and there is no other God.;
I am God, and there is none like Me.
I make known the end from the beginning,
from ancient times, what is still to come.
I say: My purpose will stand,
and I will do all that I please.
From the east, I summon a bird of prey;
from a far-off land, a man to fulfill my purpose.
What I have said, that will I bring about;
what I have planned, that will I do.
Listen to Me, you stubborn-hearted,
you who are far from righteousness.
I am bringing My righteousness near;
it is not far away,
and My salvation will not be delayed.'
(Isaiah 46:9-13)

THE HOLY SPIRIT DESCRIBES

Meeting in the War Chamber of Hell

The six cat princesses in Hell's War Chamber await Satan himself with all his pomp as he is determined to kill the seed of the woman before her seed, the Messiah, can crush his head. (Genesis 3:15)

SATAN: Satan as his custom enters six minutes late dressed in tight black velour with a red cape. He takes his place on the black onyx throne turning to Nissa bragging, "I almost killed God in the first Earth age. We will win in the end! I deceived Eve when she was alone by telling her a lie so I could get to Adam through her. Just as I planned, Adam fell *'hook, line, and sinker,'* one hundred percent (100%), *'lock, stock, and barrel.'* Adam knowingly disobeyed God and obeyed his wife. I legally became the god of this world! Adam blamed his wife and God.

356

When Eve blamed me for deceiving her to God, God took Eve's side promising her that one of her descendants would crush my head and that I would bruise his heel. (Genesis 3:15) Since then we have studied every person in the pure bloodline to determine how to defile (make unclean, corrupt) them.

My motto I present to them is, 'Have fun now, and worry about the cost later.' Offering the forbidden by God sexual pleasures outside of marriage is the easiest!

We must work in a seducing manner cunningly so the individual will not know of our activities. Keep a file of every person made in the image of God. Hit their weakness – anger, lust, resentment, stealing, worry, and murder! The big six! Once they have murdered an innocent man, they are defiled and cut off as this sin starts a strong generational curse. Most have fallen as they yield to our temptations. Marriage with Heavens blessings is our greatest enemy. 'A rope that is of three strains (husband, wife, and Jesus) is hard to break.' (Ecclesiastes 4:12)

My six cat princesses, "Where are we in destroying these humans made in the image of God?"

NISSA: Nissa briefs, "We were down to Noah on the pure bloodline! We got all the humans on Earth, but eight as the Second Earth Age ended. We pressured one of Noah's sons to commit a homosexual act when Noah was drunk. However, two sons left cleaving to their wives. Why do they like women, when men are more beautiful lovers?"

SATAN: "We must cut off that pure line! Legality, if we cut that bloodline that is it. We have won! I hate the 'unfairness' to us of God's forgiving people after they confess their sins and repent by turning away from sin. It was illegal for the 'prostitute Rahab (Hebrew 11:31), a whore, and Ruth the Moabite (Ruth 4:10), being of a nation, who practice the sacrifice of children (See 2 Kings 3:27) to idols, to be adopted into the pure lineage of the one to crush my beautiful head. We now have it narrowed down to David! One man!"

Satan questions, "Nissa, what is our plan to destroy David? I suggest homosexuality or get him to murder an innocent person. Let us work our plan to 'steal, kill, and destroy' (John 10:10) that pure bloodline."

Nissa pulls down a black curtain revealing the lineage chart from the seed of the repentant Adam starting with his and Eve's righteous son Seth. Abraham and King David are in the line of the pure seed of the woman. The Scriptures earlier said about Abraham,

THE SPIRIT OF TRUTH SINGING

'Should I hide my plan (to destroy Sodom and Gomorrah) *from Abraham?' the Lord asked. 'For Abraham will become a great and mighty nation, and all the nations of the Earth will be blessed through him. I have singled him out so he will direct his sons and their families to keep the way of the Lord by doing what is right and just. Then I will do for Abraham all that I have promised.'* (Genesis 18:17-19)

NISSA: Nissa explains, "Here are two charts. The Messiah will be the seed of the woman, but it is impossible for a woman to have a son without the sperm of a man. Right now, it has come down to David. We have a plan in place to destroy David in God's sight. Let us review the pure lineage to date:

NISSA SINGS

FROM ABRAHAM TO DAVID

'Abraham was the father of Isaac,
 Isaac the father of Jacob,
Jacob the father of Judah and his brothers,
Judah the father of Perez and Zerah, whose mother was Tamar,
Perez the father of Hezron,
Hezron the father of Ram,
Ram the father of Amminadab,
Amminadab the father of Nahshon,
Nahshon the father of Salmon,
Salmon the father of Boaz, whose mother was Rahab,
Boaz the father of Obed, whose mother was Ruth,
Obed the father of Jesse,
and Jesse the father of King David.' (Matthew 1:1-6)

FROM ADAM TO DAVID

'David, the son of Jesse,
the son of Obed, the son of Boaz,
the son of Salmon, the son of Nahshon,
the son of Amminadab, the son of Ram,
the son of Hezron, the son of Perez,
the son of Judah, the son of Jacob,
the son of Isaac, the son of Abraham,
the son of Terah, the son of Nahor,
the son of Serug, the son of Reu,
the son of Peleg, the son of Eber,
the son of Shelah, the son of Cainan,
the son of Arphaxad, the son of Shem,
the son of Noah, the son of Lamech,
the son of Methuselah, the son of Enoch,
the son of Jared, the son of Mahalalel,
the son of Cainan, the son of Enos,
the son of Melea, the son of Menna,
the son of Mattatha, the son of Nathan,
the son of David, the son of Jesse,
the son of Obed, the son of Boaz,
the son of Salmon, the son of Nahshon,
the son of Amminadab, the son of Ram,
the son of Hezron, the son of Perez,
the son of Judah, the son of Jacob,
the son of Isaac, the son of Abraham,
the son of Terah, the son of Nahor,
the son of Serug, the son of Reu,
the son of Peleg, the son of Eber,
the son of Shelah, the son of Cainan,
the son of Arphaxad, the son of Shem,
the son of Noah, the son of Lamech,
the son of Methuselah, the son of Enoch,
the son of Jared, the son of Mahalalel,
the son of Kenan,
the son of Seth, the son of Adam,
the (created out of the dust of Earth) son of God.' (Luke 3:31-38)

Nissa further explains, "It is the seed of a woman, but all these children are the result of the sperm of some man. It is a mystery indeed!
How can it be the seed of the woman when a man's sperm must fertilize the woman's egg to produce a child? Let us re-examine what our enemy God said initially:

359

NISSA SINGS

'And God said, 'Who told you (Adam) *that you were naked? Have you eaten from the tree I commanded you not to eat from?' The man said, "The woman you put here with me – she gave me some fruit from the tree, and I ate it."*

Then the Lord God said to the woman, "What is this you have done?" The woman said, "The serpent deceived me, and I ate."

So the Lord God said to the serpent, "Because you have done this,
'Cursed are you above all livestock and all wild animals!
You will crawl on your belly, and you will eat dust all the days of your life.
And I will put enmity between you and the woman,
and between your offspring and hers;
he will crush your head, and you will strike his heel.'

To the woman He said,
'I will make your pains in childbearing very severe;
with painful labor, you will give birth to children.
Your desire will be for your husband,
and he will rule over you."

To Adam he said,
"Because you listened to your wife and ate fruit from the tree about which I commanded you,
'You must not eat from it,'
'Cursed is the ground because of you;
through painful toil, you will eat food from it
all the days of your life.
It will produce thorns and thistles for you,
and you will eat the plants of the field.
By the sweat of your brow,
you will eat your food
until you (your physical body) *return to the ground,*
since from it you were taken,
for dust you are
and to dust you will return.' (Genesis 3:11-19)

Nissa observes, "It is a narrow path from the sperm of these right-eous men – Abel, Seth, Noah, Shem, Abraham, Isaac, Jacob, Judah, and now David. All our many attempts to kill King David have failed! He does not have a homosexual bone in his body!
King Saul even propositioned that he would give his daughter Michal to David as a wife if David would give him the foreskins of a hundred Philistines. (1 Samuel 18:24)

King Saul hoped that David would be killed, but David escaped death again and gave King Saul two hundred foreskins of the Philistines to win the offered prize. So King Saul had to give his daughter Michal to David as a wife.

Nevertheless, after Saul had David on the run, King Saul took Michal away from David giving her to another man, Paltiel, the son of Laish. (1 Samuel 25:44) Michal had the sexual chemistry with Paltiel, who to her looked more kingly, like her dad Saul. He had the darker skin to match her skin with David's face contrasting having a healthy ruddy, ((1 Samuel 17:42) white skin color she despised, with a hump on his nose. Michal would have her chin up in the air in pride because of her beauty in contrast to the skinny, but muscular, David, who joked and enjoyed life as a little child.

When King Saul was dead and arrived here in Hell, David still loved Michal. When David was negotiating to unite Israel under his kingship, his first requirement of Abner was that Michal should be returned to him. (See 2 Samuel 3:12-16) He finally had sex with her trying to have a baby, but Michael a cold fish could not conceive. (See 2 Samuel 6:28) She blamed David for her having no children, but she was a cold dish rag and a dry well. David had the chemistry and romantic love for her, but she despised him and even refused to kiss him. Finally, she sought to disgrace David in public as one of our loyal demons brought us a portion of the recorded event:

NISSA SINGS

'So David went to bring up the ark of God from the house of Obed-Edom to the City of David with rejoicing. When those carrying the ark of the Lord had taken six steps, he sacrificed a bull and a fattened calf. Wearing a linen ephod, David was dancing before the Lord with all his might while he and all Israel were bringing up the ark of the Lord with shouts and the sound of trumpets.

As the ark of the Lord was entering the City of David, Michal daughter of Saul watched from a window. And when she saw King David leaping and dancing before the Lord, she despised him in her heart.

They brought the ark of the Lord and set it in its place inside the tent that David had pitched for it, and David sacrificed burnt offerings and fellowship offerings before the Lord. After he had sacrificed the burnt offerings and fellowship offerings, he blessed the people in the name of the Lord Almighty. Then he gave a loaf of bread, a cake of dates, and a cake of raisins to each person in the whole crowd of Israelites, both men and women. And all the people went to their homes.

When David returned home to bless his household, Michal, daughter of Saul, came out to meet him and said, "How the king of Israel has distinguished himself today, going around half-naked in full view of the slave girls of his servants as any vulgar fellow would!"

David said to Michal, "It was before the Lord, who chose me rather than your father or anyone from his house when he appointed me ruler over the Lord's people Israel – I will celebrate before the Lord. I will become even more undignified than this, and I will be humiliated in my own eyes. But by these slave girls you spoke of, I will be held in honor.' (2 Samuel 6:12-27)

Nissa bragged, "None of the children David has now with other women can be a pure one as we have corrupted every one of them. I have a plan to corrupt David so he would also be disqualified to be in the pure line leading to the birth of the Messiah who would crush your head!"

The Father and Son Discourse on King David

FATHER: The Father God interjects, "My Son, You are going to take the punishment deserved for the upcoming gross sins of King David, and for all who will sincerely repent and receive You as Savior and confess You as their Lord."

SON: "My Father, how low will King David fall into sin?"

FATHER: "My Son, whom I love, King David is going to get prideful and commit premeditated murder of a man after he commits adultery with that man's wife. Only Your precious blood as a sacrificial *'Lamb of God,'* (John 1:29) can cover sin! 'The law came to make sin utterly sinful (with severe penalties for violation). But when sin increased, God's grace (when the sinner repented and received Jesus as Savior) abounded all the more.' (Romans 5:20) The shedding of Your Blood to forgive sins in the Age of Grace is a mystery hidden before the foundation of the world."

THE HOLY SPIRIT DESCRIBES

Nissa's Plan to Seduce and Corrupt King David to Commit Adultery and Murder

FAMILIAR SPIRIT: A familiar spirit, a fallen angel, reports to Nissa, "It's King David! If we can corrupt David, we would break the pure lineage, bloodline, from which the Messiah would be born of a woman. But, how?

NISSA: Nissa answers, "Adultery and murder! Search out the sexiest ignored married girl in Jerusalem and report back. David's marriage is on the rocks as his wife hates him and desire him dead. Go!"

FAMILIAR SPIRIT: Shortly the familiar spirits reports back, "Nissa, it's Bathsheba, the wife of Uriah, a Hittite.

NISSA: "Set the snare, trap! David has a cold and mean wife, and a Hittite has homosexual tendencies. Set the mousetrap of adultery for David and tempt him to take the sexual defilement cheese."

THE HOLY SPIRIT INTERJECTS AND SINGS

The Holy Spirit in Heaven dictates, "For the archives, the Hittites (Genesis 10:15) were from the cursed son of Canaan involved in homosexuality (Genesis 9:22-23), with Noah decreeing,

'Cursed be Canaan!
The lowest of slaves
will he be to his brothers.'
(Genesis 9:24)

The Hittite pagan practices of worshiping false gods were so corrupting that We mandated through Moses,

THE HOLY SPIRIT SINGS

'My angel will go before you and bring you into the land of (the) Canaanites, Hivites (Hittites). *Do not bow down before their* (false) *gods or worship them or follow their practices. You must demolish them* (the Hebrews did not fully obey the commandment to kill all the evil Hittites) *and break their sacred stones to pieces.'* (Exodus 23:23-24)

The Holy Spirit continues, "In a battle for territory Bathsheba, then age five and others, were captured and made slaves and bought by a wealthy Hittite. She was passed down through inheritance to rich Uriah, a Hittite. He married her when she was only twelve with the understanding that he would seek to consummate the marriage if he were back from war when she was sixteen. He has never even kissed her or slept with her.

Uriah, an expert in war, has deep-seated DNA homosexual tendencies and likes young boys. He never had a normal desire to consummate the marriage. Uriah once took an oath not to have a family if he was in the army so he would be fearless to die in battle if the line of duty so required. Bathsheba is in the pure line from Eve and Sarah. (See Matthew 1:6) She daily reads from the first five books of Moses, and is a virtuous and pure girl of prayer.

Now let us rejoin the dialog in Hell of Nissa being briefed by a research demon familiar with both Uriah and David."

FAMILIAR SPIRIT: The demon continues, "Bathsheba's husband is one of David's most loyal soldiers. She is left alone, and she likes to take a bath on Friday nights in the fresh air before an open window, which can be viewed into from a corner of the roof of the Palace. King David is usually out at war and has never gone up to this corner of the roof at night. This Friday night a full moon will shine right into Bathsheba's bathroom window."

NISSA: "Perfect! Familiar spirits, here are your assignments. First, discourage David from going off to war this week. Puff him up with pride making him feel he has earned a Spring Break. Have King Saul's daughter scorn and reject him to the uttermost. Next, you will remind David of this place on the roof from where he can observe the battle in the distance and the full moon rising. One look and we have him! Set the trap, and this is going to be easy."

ADAPTED FROM THE UNABRIDGED
www.amaxon.com Books Love & War by Joe Ragland
www.raglandministries.org/loveandwarbook/
BOOK TEN – Chapter 4

Scene Fifty-Five

King David Commits Adultery and Murder

THE HOLY SPIRIT DESCRIBES

MESSENGER: A runner from the front lines brings a message to King David reporting, "Abner has decided to attack the enemy's camp tonight from three sides at the rising of the full moon. They will be forced to flee up the ravine. As they are out of breath and are almost at the top, we have a special combat team under the leadership of Uriah, the Hittite, to cut them down."

DAVID: "Excellent plan. Uriah is one of my most loyal subjects! I will not have to be there tonight. Abner and Uriah can do it without me. What time does the full moon rise?"

MESSENGER: "It rises at 9:06 P.M. You should have an excellent view from your roof of the horizon. You might, if the wind is just right, even hear the sounds of our attack."

DAVID: "Tell the men their king will be watching the horizon. I almost wish I could be with you tonight."

MESSENGER: "Sir, you could surprise the men and ride back with me!"

DAVID: "It is a thought, but my wife Michal is looking exceedingly beautiful today. I might with a little luck even talk her into going up on the roof with me to watch the full moon rise and listen to the battle. It is written and sung about some past moonlight romances,

DAVID SINGS

"Salmon was the father of Boaz,
Whose mother was Rahab (a forgiven harlot; Joshua 2).
Boaz was the father of Obed,
Whose mother was Ruth (a forgiven Moabite; Ruth 4:13-22)
Obed was the father of Jesse,
And Jesse was the father of King David,
David was the father of (Unidentified at this time.)"
(See Matthew 15-6)

Something romantic often happens in the moonlight. Why shouldn't the most beautiful woman in the kingdom, the daughter of King Saul, my wife Michal, be the mother of our next King, from whose bloodline the Messiah will be born crushing the head of the devil?"

MESSENGER: "I have not seen my wife now in three months. I must get back to the battle line. We need every man at his post this evening as we *'acknowledge the Lord in all our ways.'* (Proverbs 3:5-6)

DAVID: David continues to anticipate romancing in the marriage bed all afternoon with his wife, he considers the most beautiful woman in the world. David bathes himself and puts on a soft blue robe singing,

DAVID SINGING

"This is better than army gear. Michal will like the feel of this. Saul sure had a beautiful daughter. I won her as a prize when I killed Goliath. Tonight she might finally get pregnant. I would like to have a son, an heir, from a wife I love. I like these practice sessions with her."

MAID: David goes to Michal's quarters, and her maid announces, "Your husband David is here!"

MICHAL: Michal replies to the house cleaner, "He is no husband. It's my monthly time!"

Michal walks out looking more beautiful than ever declaring, "Dave, the men are all off to war! They need you at the helm of the ship. What are you doing in that sissy outfit with your snow-white hairy skinny legs showing?

No, I am not interested! It is my time of the month! (Lying) After your disrobing childish dance you put on in front of the women, I have decided to let you have relations with Abigal, whom you took as a wife after her husband came against you and died. King Saul took me away from you and gave me as wife to Paltiel, (1 Samuel 25:44)

Abigal, has gained a lot of weight and has a few white hairs, but she still has some fire in the basement. (Smirking)

Besides, I also have a headache! (Lying) I thought you were off at battle protecting the country. You were the last person I expected to see walk in here tonight. I have given up trying to have a baby with you. My dad, King Saul had given me to another husband, Paltiel, and he is the only man I love. I am married to him and not to skinny ruddy you. I wear only his wedding ring. You do not look like a king - white baby face, skinny, with a humped nose.

I suggest you do what you do best - kill Philistines. Goodnight and goodbye!"

Michal turns her head and walks away not looking back with her maid shaking her head and closing the door in King David's face. That night, having taken herself out from under her husband's covering of protection, the evil demon spirits of cancer entered her female parts and she died in 66 days and 6 hours from the time she humiliated and shamed David by refusing to give him the marriage romantic intimacy rights he was begging from his wife. As Michal lay dying, she sang,

MICHAL DYING SONG

'Husband, who do you think you are?
My body is mine alone and not yours.
I refuse to be a sex slave in marriage.
Commit adultery if you must.
The bottom line is don't sexually harass me.
I had rather die than submit to a husband I hate!'

THE SPIRIT OF TRUTH SINGS

"Forever, O Lord (Jesus is Lord) Your Word (recorded
in the Bible) is settled in Heaven.

"Your Word is a lamp to my feet, and a
Light (showing me God's will) to my path.

"Establish my steps and direct them by
(truths in) Your Word; let not any
sin control (have dominion over) me."
(Psalm 119:89, 105. 133)

"For with God nothing is ever impossible, and no
Word from God shall be without power or impossible of fulfillment. "
(Luke 1:37)

366

DAVID ON THE HARP SINGS

Michal's response was rejection, contempt, scorn, indifference, and separation. She indicates she is in love with Paltiel after King Saul slandered me and gave her to Paltiel as his wife. "My mind remains in a fog. The one time I needed Michal; she denied me my marital right. I put all my chemistry eggs in her one basket. There is nothing as useless as a wife who hates her husband. All I have is a backup, wife, Abigail, to which I have little chemistry. Abigail has gained so much weight and was so abused by an evil husband. Let me go up to the roof and listen to the battle as the full moon rises."

HOLY SPIRIT DESCRIBES

David pulls up a light chair and sits in the corner of the roof awaiting the moon rise. Just as the moon breaks the darkness with a brilliant fullness, David hears the clash of armor in the distance. Then David looks down through a small opening on the edge of the roof and sees a purple curtain partly open.

The most beautiful young girl, even more beautiful than Michal, he has ever seen was in a bathtub with bubbles up to her chin joyfully laughing and blowing bubbles out the slightly open window. One bubble floats up and burst on David's lips. Her maid with a large sea sponge washes her back. She then lies back, pushing her small pointed breast slightly out of the water into the moonlight with the maid circling each, which makes the nipples more erect. At this stage, that was not the only thing erect. David was breathing hard, hoping they would not hear him gasping at such a beautiful sight. David reasons, *"If I can breathe a little quieter, she has to stand up!"*

Then the young girl lays back again, pulling her small pointed breasts back beneath the water and resting her head back on a soft folded towel. It seemed like forever as the steam was rising all around her from the hot colds keeping her tub warm. Finally, David heard the pleasant female laughing saying, "Please bring me some rinse water, a drying towel, and hand me the sponge for me to wash my womanly parts." As the girl stands up with bubbles all over her tiny pointed breasts, David saw her perfectly shaped pubic hair. The girl circles her flat stomach and navel with a sponge and turns her back to him as she soaps her female parts. The rinse water was poured over her shoulders and then over each shapely leg. She stepped out of the tub into a fluffy white towel with David's breathing growing louder and louder as he grew harder and harder thinking, *"Those are the most beautiful legs in the world. I would love to penetrate . . . . **Only if I am married to her!**"* David's breathing grows even louder. The girl shouts, "Did you hear something? Shut the drape!" As the curtain was closed, David noticed, that some semen had leaked from his erection giving him a little relief.

David finally falls to sleep and awakens in the morning, having dreamed of the laughing beautiful girl, distracting him from giving his usual thanksgiving, praise, and worship to the Lord. He strums his love for the mysterious joyful stranger on his harp.

DAVID SINGS AND PLAYS THE HARP

'Some Anointed Evening I have seen a stranger,
I have heard her laughing across a great divide.

And night after night, as strange as it seems,
The sound of her laughter will sing in my dreams.

Some anointed evening, when I find my true love,
I'll fly to her side and make her my own,
or throughout my life, I may dream of such romance all alone.

Once I have found her, I'll never let her go.'

(Adapted from *Some Enchanted Evening* in the movie "*South Pacific*" written by Rodgers and Hammerstein)

"I've got to have that beautiful stranger for my wife!
Eve could not have been more beautiful!
She is more beautiful than my wife Michal, who has rejected me.
What a delightful and joyful laugh."

DAVID: David dressed and ran outside the palace, to the house on the street where she lives. He passes a beggar, who had slept on the street asking, "Whose house is that?"

BEGGAR: "King David that is your trusted captain Uriah's house he inherited from his wealthy Hittite father."

DAVID: "Does he have a daughter?"

BEGGAR: "No, but he robbed the cradle and has a very young wife girl."

DAVID: David inquired further, "Would you by chance know Uriah's wife's name?"

BEGGAR: "No, I don't know her name. I know she is married to the bravest man, beside you, in the kingdom. She frequently places a coin in my cup and speaks a kind word over me. She has even sent her maid out to give others and myself, freshly baked bread and fruit. Her consideration of the poor is why I have chosen to sit on the street where she lives. There is not a more compassionate damsel in all Jerusalem!"

DAVID: David returns to the palace and brings in his trusted advisor and propositioned, "What would you think about honoring our men on the front lines? I could by executive order declare Army Day as a national holiday. I thought about a military wife to head this up. What about Uriah's wife?

TRUSTED ADVISOR: "Yes, I met her once. There is not a kinder and pure young lady in the Kingdom. She was born of godly parents with her bloodline being traced back to Sarah and Seth."

DAVID: "What is her name?"

TRUSTED ADVISOR: "I do not know, but I will find out for you. This afternoon we are honoring some widows here in the palace, and would you like me to ask Uriah's wife to help in this honoring. She could give words of comfort as her husband is so important to our defense and he is always away."

DAVID: "Yes, send for her and tell her to prepare words of comfort for our military widows. Find out her name. We will meet in the Grand Hall at 7:00 P.M. this evening. Come and find me when everything is in place to formally introduce us."

TRUSTED ADVISOR: Following the program in which Uriah's wife addressed the war widows with the utmost compassion, received this introduction to her King, "King David, this is Uriah's wife, who is fighting even this night to protect our country."

DAVID: King David, not acknowledging the Lord, indicates to that he desires her to stay for him to talk with her about Army Day as a national holiday and for him to show her something special. David walks her up to the roof saying, "The full moon is about to rise and listen carefully, and you can hear the battle. Your husband studies and lives for war. How did a daughter of Sarah marry a Hittite? How old are you? Eighteen? Will you at least tell me your name and its meaning even in song?

BATHSHEBA RESPECTFULLY SINGS

'My King, my name is Bathsheba,
from the Hebrew meaning 'daughter of an oath,'
referring to the oath God gave Eve after the devil had deceived her, promising
"one of her descendants (the Messiah) will crush the head of the devil,
and the devil will bruise His (the Messiah's) heel.
(Genesis 3:15)

Today is my birthday, and I am sixteen.
My parents were slaves of a rich Hittite, and I was an inheritance left in a
'Will' to Uriah, with the lovely house and other riches next door.
It seems the only thing this Hittite likes is war as he has studied war from a child.
You are his hero after you killed Goliath, and was rewarded the most
beautiful woman in the realm for a wife as a reward by King Saul.
Uriah when home, sleeps with a chamber boy,
And he has never slept with or kissed me. '

DAVID: David squares off to look into Bathsheba's beautiful face and eyes just as the moon rises, saying, "You and I have a problem in common - cold rejecting spouses! Let me show you something."

BATHSHEBA: David takes Bathsheba by the hand and walks over to the corner of the roof with Bathsheba gasping when she sees her bathtub in the light of the moon apologizing, "I had no idea! I thought I heard something. I am so sorrow! Forgive me, my King. I forget I am no longer a child as my breasts are so small."

DAVID: "But very beautiful and breathtaking in the moonlight!"

BATHSHEBA: "I must go! Forgive me. I didn't know you were here."

DAVID PICKS UP HIS HARP AND AGAIN SINGS

'Some Anointed Evening I may see a stranger,
I may hear her laughing across a great divide.

And night after night, as strange as it seems,
The sound of her laughter will sing in my dreams.

Some anointed evening, when you find your true love,
fly to her side and make her your own,
or throughout your life you may dream all alone.

Once I have found her, I'll never let her go!'
(Adapted from *Some Enchanted Evening* in the movie "*South Pacific*" written by Rodgers and Hammerstein)

David takes her other hand holding them firmly looking her in the eyes quickly and tenderly kissing her on the lips asking, "Is that okay?"

BATHSHEBA: "A kiss from my king is 'better than okay,' but you must let me go, as this is forbidden fruit under the law as we are both married. I am a virgin, and I am saving myself for Uriah, my husband as he indicated that he would consummate our marriage when I was sixteen, which should be the next time he returns from battle. However, he does not seem to have any affection for me.

I have caught him a few times with two young naked sons of our servants. He would have one of the boy's private part in his mouth, and the other naked boy would have his private part in his mouth. He once indicated that he was a descendant of Ham, who I understand also liked young boys."

DAVID: David on his right knee asked, "If you become a widow, like all those here tonight, would you consider marrying me?"

BATHSHEBA: "Yes, after the customary time of mourning."

DAVID: David again pulls her up to him, saying, "Another kiss to seal what will be our future marriage covenant!"
While they were kissing, David with one hand unties the left bow to her robe, slips his hand into her loose robe with her not wearing a bra, and takes her left small-pointed breast in his hands Breathing hard, he responds, "Preview of future marriage attractions! Bathsheba, I am going to marry you some way!" David then unties the right bow, letting her robe drop to the floor with her wearing white bikini panties. David, removing his shirt suggests, "Let's go over to the chaise lounge, and you can lie back on my shoulder. I have a light blanket and a pillow."

BATHSHEBA: Bathsheba, resting her head on David's bare shoulder replies, "This is far enough! Let us wait! The Lord will make a way for us both to be free for marriage, without committing adultery, which would be a great sin against God. I will make you a warm and a loving wife. Be patient like Job! God will make a way!"

DAVID: '*It can't be wrong when it feels so right.*' (Quoting an often untruth from the song '*You Light Up My Life*' by Joe Brooks sung by Debby Boone.)

BATHSHEBA: Bathsheba urges, "My King, it is wrong as our God commands, '*Thou shalt not commit adultery*!' (Exodus 20:14) It would defile us both. Please don't!"

DAVID: David breathes hard kissing her on the mouth and breasts saying, "Anything more than a mouthful is a waste!" David ever so gently slips his hand inside her panties, feeling her dripping wet with her starting to move against his hand. He takes her hand and places it on the rise in his pants with her squeezing it. David said, "Let me just rub the head up and down."

Soon David, breathing hard, had difficulty breaking her hymen with Bathsheba also breathing hard helping him push. Soon David is in, and a few ins and outs he fills her vagina with sperm. David and Bathsheba fall asleep in the moonlight under a light blanket with David still in her. David awakens with the first light of dawn with his erection growing again. As Bathsheba awakens, she naturally kisses him passionately with David taking his time so slowly, and when he brings Bathsheba first to an organism, he starts moving and fills her vagina with sperm for the second time.

David, staying inside her for a few minutes, explains, "We have to get you home or both our names will be 'mud.' My head has not been this clear in years! I must have had a lot of toxins I needed to release."

David looks down seeing all the blood indicating, "Don't move as I have a wash basin and towels near, and I will bring you a wet and a dry towel."

Bathsheba turns the chaise lounge pillows over so as not to reveal all the blood and deposits the used towels in a large basket. David, ever so gently, walks Bethesda down the back steps to the side remote door saying,
"Here is a private key to this side door. Please come for dinner at 7:00 P.M. this evening to the King's Private Dining Room one floor below this roof as my servants are sworn to absolute secrecy. Wear something comfortable and casual. I truly love you, my darling!

I have never seen anything so lovely as the way you looked tonight. Come 'Hell or high water,' I will marry you!"

BATHSHEBA: "Please don't use that word 'Hell' as I am scared of that horrible place. We have defiled ourselves, and have sinned greatly against our loving and merciful God."

BEGGAR: David kisses Bathsheba romantically on her perfectly shaped lips with his kisses being returned. David opens the door with the same beggar holding out his cup, saying, "Good morning, King David. Your secret is secure with me! I could hear some of your talking last evening from the roof." Bathsheba drops a coin in the beggar's cup without a word and enters her house

THE HOLY SPIRIT DESCRIBES

URIAH: Bathsheba during her usual afternoon nap has a dream. In her dream, she is carrying a male baby in her arms, and when walking through a field of battle, she sees her husband Uriah lying back mortally wounded, who screams out, "Adulterer! Bastard baby! I put you under a curse by my god Baal, who gave you to me. I wish my god Baal had given me a young boy instead of you. Hell has won, and you are defiled forever! You have been eliminated from the pure line of the seed of a woman to give birth to the Messiah. Defiled forever!"

BATHSHEBA: Uriah close to breathing what appears to be his last breath, with Bathsheba responding, '*No weapon formed against me shall prosper*!' (Isaiah 54:17) I am not under your curse for '*the blood of Jesus, God's Son, purifies me from every sin.*' (1 John 1:7) I decree our marriage is annulled, for it was never consummated at no fault of mine!"

URIAH: Uriah looks down seeing coming up out of the ground two hideous demons to take him to Hell as he was dying he screams, "Baal, you lied to me! You promised me, sixty-six young boys, with which to have oral and anal sex." The demons sneer at Bathsheba and take Uriah's spirit and throw it into the fires of Hell where other demons torture him."

THE HOLY SPIRIT SINGS
JERUSALEM POST REPORTS

"Queen Michal, thirty-six, died Saturday evening after a painful bout with cancer. She is buried beside the ashes of her father, the late King Saul, the first King of Israel. King David had won Michal as a prize for killing Goliath. However, King Saul, later gave his daughter, Michal, to be the wife of another man causing further friction without legally divorcing David. David, also lost his wife Abigail earlier this year, leaving the Kingdom today without a queen. David indicated that it was until death they parted, and he was glad he had no son as an heir to the throne of either Michal or Abigail.

Michal and Abigail's fortunes have been donated by King David to the new '*Army Widows' Relief Fund*' headed by Uriah the Hittite's wife, who recently also became a widow, to take care of destitute war widows and children.

David also indicated he is gathering the building material for a New Temple. David reports that since he is a man of war, a future unknown son would build God's Temple, bringing in great peace and prosperity for Israel. **Query:** Could this unknown future son of David be the long-awaited Messiah of Israel to kill all our enemies?"

THE SPIRIT OF TRUTH FROM GOD'S WORD SINGS

The Holy Spirit dictates into the achieves the recording in Heaven's account of David's act of adultery and premeditated murder,
'In the spring, when kings go off to war, David sent Joab out with the king's men and the whole Israelite army. They destroyed the Ammonites and besieged Rabbah. But David remained in Jerusalem. One evening David got up from his bed and walked around on the roof of the palace.
From the roof, he saw a woman bathing. The woman was very beautiful and exquisite, and David sent someone to find out about her. The man said, 'She is Bathsheba, the daughter of Eliam and the wife of Uriah the Hittite.'

Then David sent messengers to get her. She came to him, and he slept with her. (Now she was purifying herself from her monthly uncleanness.) Then she went back home. The woman conceived, and sent word to David, saying, "I am pregnant."

So David sent this word to Joab: "Send me Uriah the Hittite." And Joab sent him to David. When Uriah came to him, David asked him how Joab was, how the soldiers were, and how the war was going. Then David said to Uriah, "Go down to your house and wash your feet." So Uriah left the palace, and a gift from the king was sent after him. But Uriah slept at the entrance to the palace with all his master's servants, and did not go down to his house.

David was told, 'Uriah did not go home.' So he asked Uriah, 'Haven't you just come from a military campaign? Why didn't you go home?'

Uriah said to David, "The ark and Israel and Judah are staying in tents, and my commander Joab, and my lord's men are camped in the open country. How could I go to my house to eat, drink, and lie with my wife? As surely as you live, I will not do such a thing!" Then David said to him, "Stay here one more day, and tomorrow I will send you back." So Uriah remained in Jerusalem that day and the next. At David's invitation, he ate and drank with him, and David made him drunk. But in the evening Uriah went out to sleep on his mat among his master's servants; he did not go home.

In the morning, David wrote a letter to Joab, and sent it (sealed) with Uriah. In it, he wrote, 'Put Uriah out in front where the fighting is fiercest. Then withdraw (premeditated murder) from him so he will be struck down and die.'

So while Joab had the city under siege, he put Uriah, where he knew the strongest defenders were. When the men of the city came out and fought against Joab, some men in David's army fell; moreover, Uriah the Hittite was dead. Joab sent David a full account of the battle. He instructed the messenger: 'When you have finished giving the king this account of the battle the king's anger may flare up, and he may ask you, 'Why did you get so close to the city to fight? Did not you know they would shoot arrows from the wall? Who killed Abimelech, son of Jerub-Besheth[¡]? Did not a woman drop an upper millstone on him from the wall, so he died in Thebez? Why did you get so close to the wall?' If he asks you this, then say to him 'Moreover, your servant Uriah the Hittite is dead.'

The messenger set out, and when he arrived, he told David everything Joab had sent him to say. The messenger said to David, 'The men overpowered us and came out against us in the open, but we drove them back to the entrance of the city gate. Then the archers shot arrows at your servants from the wall, and some of the king's men died. Moreover, your servant Uriah the Hittite is dead.'

David told the messenger, 'Say this to Joab: 'Don't let this upset you; the sword devours one as well as another. Press the attack against the city and destroy it.' Say this to encourage Joab."

When Uriah's wife heard that her husband was dead, she mourned for him. After the time of mourning was over, David had her brought to his house, and she became his wife and bore him a son. But the thing David had done (adultery and premeditated murder) displeased the Lord.' (2 Samuel 11:1-27)

NATHAN SONG OF REBUKE TO DAVID

'So why did you ignore the Lord's command
(not to commit adultery and murder)?
So why did you do what God says is wrong?
You struck down (murdered) Uriah the Hittite with the sword
of the Ammonites and took his wife to be your own.
Now, therefore, the sword will never depart (in your lifetime) from your house,
because you despised Me and took the wife of Uriah the Hittite to be your own.'
(2 Samuel 12:9-10)

King David's Repentance

David loses his joy and enters deep remorse for his gross sins after Nathan the Prophet comforts him regarding his sins of adultery and murder with David finally repenting and singing in prayer,

KING DAVID SINGS HIS PRAYER OF REPENTANCE

'Have mercy on me, O God,
according to Your unfailing love;
according to Your great compassion
blot out my transgressions.
Wash away all my guilt
and make me clean again from my sin.
Give me back the joy of Your salvation!

Keep me strong by giving me a willing spirit.
Then I will teach Your ways to those who do wrong,
and sinners will turn back [repent] *to You.*
God, save me from the guilt of murder,
God of my salvation (rescue me)*,*
and I will sing (for joy) *about your goodness.*
Lord, let me speak so I may praise You.
. . . Do whatever good You wish for Jerusalem.

Then there were righteous sacrifices (with the blood of bulls
rolling sins forward until the Lamb of God can be slain,
shedding His blood for the sins of those who will receive Him as Savior)*.'*
(Psalm 51:1-2, 9-15, 18)

THE SPIRIT OF TRUTH SINGS

Then David (in deep repentance) said to Nathan,
'I have sinned (greatly) against the Lord.'
Nathan (a prophet speaking for God) answered,
'The Lord has taken away (forgiven) your sin.
You will not die (Psalm 51 repentance, followed by grace). But what
you did (choosing to disobey the commandments of
God to not commit adultery and to not murder) caused
the Lord's enemies to lose respect) for the Lord. For this
reason the son (baby) who was born to you will die.'

DAVID SINGS

"While the baby was still alive, I fasted, and
I cried (in prayer). I thought, 'Who knows?
Maybe the Lord will feel sorry for me and let the
baby live.' But now that the baby is dead, why
should I fast? I can't bring him back to life.
someday I will go to him (in Paradise)
bute cannot come to me.
Then David comforted (assuring her, she also
Was forgiven) Bathsheba his wife. He had
(romantic) sexual relations with her.

She became pregnant again and had another son,
whom David named Solomon. The Lord loved
(being in the pure bloodline, for the future birth of the
Seed of the woman to crush the devil's head) Solomon. "
(2 Samuel 12:22-24)

BATHSHEBA'S SONG OF PRAISE
UPON THE BIRTH OF SOLOMON

"Our good, merciful, and gracious Father, in Heaven.
I bestow a smiling kiss of blessing and dedication on our son,
Solomon, conceived in great love between a husband and wife.
I consecrate Solomon as part of the bloodline of the Messiah.
The devil meant all this shame for evil, but Father You will work it
all for the good of Your glorious Kingdom of Love.
While my name among the people stands for adulterous woman
and mother of a bastard baby, I trust in
Your timing in Eternity to take away my shame.
May Solomon have so many children that Hell is in
confusion and defeat in seeking to destroy the pure bloodline of the Messiah.
While my name is scorned on Earth, I will honour the Lord, throughout
Eternity, for using this humble handmaiden in the bloodline of the Messiah.
Thank You that my husband and that I have been forgiven for much
For whom much has been forgiven, loves much!
Please grant our son of love, Solomon, wisdom, unequalled until the
Messiah is born of a woman, and crushes the head of the devil.
Thank You for my having come into Your glorious kingdom for such a time as this
to raise Solomon, who is the great-grandfather of the Messiah.
In the Name of the Messiah, Jesus, Amen!
Hallelujah!"

The Devil Mocking Believing the Pure Bloodline Is Finally **Defiled**

SATAN: The devil with an evil mocking brags, "Nissa, I believe you have corrupted the seed of Eve as Heaven has been silent for some time. No crushing of my head! We will win in the end as I have a better plan than I had in Atlantis to murder the Godhead. I will be worshiped as god. Do you believe me?"

NISSA: "Yes, master, Heaven is silent knowing we won. I think I have either corrupted or murdered all the seed of David. However, my assigned demon has just brought me this found recorded Scripture about Solomon:

'King Solomon, however, loved many foreign women besides Pharaoh's daughter — Moabites, Ammonites, Edomites, Sidonians, and Hittites. They were from nations about which the Lord had told the Israelites, "You must not intermarry with them because they will surely turn your hearts after their gods." Nevertheless, Solomon held fast to them in love. He had seven hundred wives of royal birth and three hundred concubines, and his (foreign) wives led him astray. As Solomon grew old, his wives turned his heart after other gods, and his heart was not wholly devoted to the Lord his God, as the heart of David his father had been. He followed Ashtoreth, the goddess of the Sidonians, and Molek, the detestable god of the Ammonites. So Solomon did evil in the eyes of the Lord; he did not follow the Lord completely, as David his father had done.

On a hill east of Jerusalem, Solomon built a high place for Chemosh the detestable god of Moab, and for Molek, the detestable god of the Ammonites. He did the same for all his foreign wives, who burned incense and offered sacrifices to their gods.

The Lord became angry with Solomon because his heart had turned away from the Lord, the God of Israel, who had appeared to him twice. Although he had forbidden Solomon to follow other gods, Solomon did not keep the Lord's command. So the Lord said to Solomon, "Since this is your attitude and you have not kept My covenant and My decrees, which I commanded you, I will most certainly tear the kingdom away from you and give it to one of your subordinates. Nevertheless, for the sake of David, your father, I will not do it during your lifetime. I will tear it out of the hand of your son. Yet I will not tear the whole kingdom from him, but will give him one tribe for the sake of David, My servant and for the sake of Jerusalem, which I have chosen.' (1 Kings 11:1-1)

Nissa asks Lucifer, the devil, "Where is Solomon? We were not watching him on his death bed. Surely, he can't be hiding out with King David over in Paradise. I corrupted him with these foreign women with his worshiping false gods. God is not fair if He forgave him on his deathbed! Like Moses, he disobeyed. We also should have had Moses!

Where are Solomon's children of those 700 wives and 300 concubines, which I call porcupines? That was a lot of children to keep up with, and we may have temporally lost a few?"

The Devil Angrily Rambles

SATAN CHANTS

SATAN: The devil in angry fury shouts, "What! You stupid fool you might have missed a few children! Kill every future baby and grandbaby. How can you be in such confusion and ignorance? Kill them all!

My scientists to destroy the Godhead are working on additional plans. I have never seen God the Father nor God the Holy Spirit.

They are hearsay from God the Son, Jesus, who says I am the first creation that existed! Jesus is no match for me. I can destroy skinny Jesus with one hand tied behind my back. I can trick Him into destroying Himself. I can fool anybody. Look how easily I deceived Eve!

I never saw God the Father nor God the Holy Spirit, and I doubt their existence. Who knows, they may have been killed in my first attack in Atlantis. I don't see how the Son escaped as the Ice Bomb blew up right on him causing the ice age.

How can God the Father exist forever? Impossible! He must be dead! If I can kill the Son, that will be it, and all the inheritance is mine. All I ever heard was thunder. I have only seen Jesus. If Jesus comes as the seed of a woman, all we have to do is to get him to sin one time, and then we would have a legal right to murder him. Simple!

Nissa, you surely will have a sexy evil woman out there to cause Jesus, the Son of God, in the flesh to be tempted and yield to sin. You can do it!

Look how you tempted Solomon. God commanded him not to marry foreign women, and he loved sex. Those 700 wives and 300 concubines (1 Kings 11:1-9.), which you call porcupines, caused him to sin greatly in his old age. Where is Solomon as I know we defiled him with great sin?

I would like to look over into Paradise, but the angels have me blocked. I have a plan to blow it up. My scientists are working on it."

The devil screams, "Where is Solomon?"

THE SPIRIT OF TRUTH SINGS

'*The Lord laughs at the wicked, for He knows their day* (of destruction) *is coming.*'
(Psalm 37:13)

FATHER: The Father smiles, explaining, "Yes, My Son, Solomon had a deathbed sincere repentance as he pled the future blood You will shed for His sins, and for all who will receive You as Savior. I forgave Solomon, and now Hell cannot locate all his seeds." (Laughter)

Solomon's Son, Rehoboam, was overlooked by Hell

Father God explains, "My Son, the seed the devil's crew missed was Rehoboam (See Matthew 1:7), whose father was Solomon. The covenant seed from the woman's pure bloodline is My daughter, Mary, a virgin, a daughter of David through his son Solomon. The devil and his crew didn't understand the need for a virgin birth, nor Your legally having to shed Your life's blood for the forgiveness of sins for all who would receive You as Savior.

Mary knew she was in the pure bloodline from Seth and was hoping and praying she might be chosen as the mother of the Messiah!

Sincerely Agape Yours,

Joe M. Ragland

Soli Deo Gloria

[*Soli Deo Gloria* is a Latin term for Glory to God alone. The phrase became one of the five solas propounded to summarize the Reformers' basic beliefs in Jesus as Savior and Lord during the Protestant Reformation. Artists have used it such as Johann Sebastian Bach, George Frederic Handel, and Christioh Grouper to signify that the work was produced for the sake of praising and hallelujah to God].

Abigail – A midwife to Mary, the mother of Jesus.

Adonis – Name means handsome and he was the youngest son of Atlas who died.

Atlas – King of City of Atlas and Atlantis.

Ape men (Ape women, Ape-men, Ape-boy) – apelike beings that have distinctly human traits.

Atlanteans – The people of Atlantis.

Ben – The one who drove Mary to Elizabeth.

Benedick – He leaked Diamond Mine Secret in the First Earth Age and was executed

Black Granite Volcano Mountain – This was located on the North side of the Island of Atlantis.

Captain Capp – He escorted the Apostle John to the Island of Patmos.

Casper – He was the one who attacked Mary in the cave.

Charity – Noah's wife, with her name meaning, "love, affection."

City of Loveland – A lovely place on the north end of Island of Atlantis.

Clara – The one who tried to seduce Jesus, and upon being saved her name was changed to Clare.

Colossus – The first Treasurer of Atlantis.

Diotrephes – The Administrator of the Church stealing from the offerings.

Dionysus – The captain of the orchestra in Heaven.

Elvis– A singer at the Marriage Supper of the Lamb (Jesus).

Familiar– A chief acquainted demon, tempting Lazarus not to correct an accounting error.

Fluffy – Eve's pet lamb. Also, the name David gave for his pet lamb. Sar, a lion, and Phar, a bear, both attacked Fluffy, and David killed them and rescued Fluffy.

Gehen – The one who killed Benedick and gambled with Atlas.

Giggala – Isaac's guardian angel.

Grant – Job's first wife's father.

Hell – A chamber in the heart of the Earth referred to by Apollyon Lucifer as his **Hab**itation for **E**cstasy in **L**ushness and **L**aciviousness (HELL)!

Harp – It is a creeping serpent having many colors going through its scales.

Hexagon Room – Atlas II's office in Atlantis.

Hodie – Atlas II's new director of the Young Boys Club to take Newton's place.

Homo – Foreman of Black Mountain Mine with Ham as his dad.

Homoper – Job defeated him in his attack and plans to murder one of Job's client's daughter, Joyce.

Sedu and Pervert – They joined in an attempt to sexually abuse and then to murder Joyce.

Hump – The name of a camel of Joyce, second wife of Job.

Imrie – Job's landowner friend attending Nissa and Job's wedding.

Jabus – One who owned the green grassy hill in the center of the fields in which the feeding of the 5,000 took place.

Jesus – The Son of God, Messiah, who died on a cross to pay the penalty for sins of those who receive Him as Savior. The Bridegroom at the wedding supper and marriage of the Lamb of God.

Jesex – Judas' wife at the First Earth Age.

Joel–The dad of Joyce, the second wife of Job.

Job – Atlas' Attorney. In the First Age.   Job's law partner in the First Earth Age was Luther.

John the Baptist – He came in the spirit and power of Elijah, preparing the way for the Messiah, Jesus, the Son of God.

Joseph of Arimathea – He donated his own prepared tomb for the burial of Jesus after Jesus' crucifixion. He asked Pilate for the body of Jesus. Joseph and Nicodemus took the body of Jesus, wrapped it in fine linen, and applied myrrh and aloes Nicodemus had bought.

Joyce – Job's second wife.

Judas Ben – The husband of Martha, sister of Lazarus.

Kosher Cuisine Red Heifer Restaurant – A business opened by Martha, the sister of Lazarus, and her husband, in Tel Aviv, Israel.

Lazarus – A friend of Jesus, and his sister are named Mary, and Martha.

Levia – Job's young pet of the sea.

Leviathans – Sea monsters in the First Earth Age referred to in the Book of Job.

Lesb – Lesbian lover to Job's first wife in the Second Earth Age.

Lucifer Apollyon – Originally the song leader of Heaven, who started receiving worship himself. He declared war on God and was cast out of Heaven to the Earth. He became the devil and deceived Eve and tempted Jesus. He murdered Jesus on a cross and Jesus legally crushed his head when He declared, "It is finished." The devil and his followers will in the end be legally cast into a Lake of Fire.

Luther – Pastor in Atlantis, and his daughter, Ruth, married Newton in the First Earth Age.

Mary Magdalene – Atlas II's director of the Young Girls Club. She was present at Jesus' crucifixion and resurrection. She was among the first to testify of Jesus' resurrection from the dead.

Melchizedek – Jesus, the Evangelist, holding a revival in this name in the First Earth Age.

Mercury – A messenger angel used by Lucifer.

Newton – Atlas II's first director of the Young Boys Club converted and chose to use his first name, John, which means "God is gracious."

Nicodemus –A member of the Sanhedrin. He visited Jesus at night to discuss Jesus' teachings. He helped prepare the body of Jesus for burial.

Nickelodeon – A temple prostitute, who later escorts Nissa in Hell.

Nissa – Job's first wife in the Second Earth Age. Used in Hell as a queen of darkness.

Ollie Marie – Chosen as a wife for Thomas, who became an Apostle. Her mother was Zuda.

Opt – Lived in Jer and was the widowed father of John Mark, who wrote the second book of the New Testament bearing his name. .

Orichal (Orichalcum) – A mixture of copper and zinc metal alloy, resembling gold, found in Atlantis.

Orphean – Apollyon Lucifer's gifted harpist.

Ped – A peddler who helped Abigail, a Shepherd, and his daughter escape from Bethlehem.

Pechblend – From which uranium (uranite) is extraced.

Pervert –Job knocked his front teeth out when he came against Job seeking to kill him with a dagger.

Phileo – Adam's pet lamb; later made by God into a coat of skin after Adam choose to sin.

Photon – Apollyon Lucifer's Chief Scientist.

Pilate – Roman ordering the crucifixion of Jesus and placed the words in three languages, "King of the Jews" above Jesus' head on the cross.

Poseidon – The name of the false god of the ocean.

Python – The name of the serpent in the Garden of Eden.

Reg – The one who registered Joseph in Bethlehem.

Safari – The wife of King Atlas.

Saul Paulos – He later became the Apostle Paul. Saul as a Roman citizen also bore the name in Greek, Paulos, and in Latin, Paulus. See **Paul the Apostle** in **Wikipedia, The Free Encyclopedia**.

Sedu – He sought to rape and then murder Joyce, with Job defending her.

Sensi – Lot's first wife on Earth, later in Hell.

Serpenies and Opthidia – Snake type demons in Hell.

Tibetan – Atlas II's Treasurer

Zeus, and Hera – Homosexual dates as rewards in First Earth Age.

Uz – The father of Attorney Job in the Second Earth Age.

VISA and VISA 666 – Names used to denote the finalization of a plan of darkness. A way of saying 'done' or 'bye' on the side of darkness, and pridefully standing for **V**ery, **I**mportant **S**upreme, **A**chiever of Apollyon.

Vampire Room – A meeting Room in Hell.

Vulcan – Atlas II's Secretary of War.

Wheel of Fortune – A gambling device in Atlas II's casino.

William Whitestone –The attorney, who train Job in the Second Earth Age to be a lawyer.

Woe and Moe – Two hideous creatures in Hell.

Zaharwandad, Hormizd, and Ariho –Names of the three wise men who brought gifts to the young child Jesus to help provide the financial means to make an emergency escape into Egypt and to finance the ministry of Jesus.

HALLELUJAH, JESUS

(A Paraphrase of Psalm 23)

Lyrics by Joe M. Ragland

Resignation, American folk melody

1. My ___ Shep - herd sup - plies ___ all I ___ need, Lord Je - sus
2. When I walk ___ through ___ the threats of ___ death, His pre - sence
3. My ___ Lord's pro - vi - sions and love fol-low me, all ___ my a -

is ___ His Name. In pas - tures green, I rest and ___ feed, ___ a - long-
gives me pro - tect - ion. ___ His ___ Shep - herd's staff and com - fort-ing rod, de - li - vers
bun - dant life days. ___ His e - ter - nal ___ house will be my ___ glee, with Hal - le -

side a peace - ful stream. ___ And when I ___ stray, ___ He brings me ___
me with no ___ re - ject - ion. ___ He fa - vors me in the sight of my
lu - jah, Je - sus I pray! ___ He brings me to ___ a glor - ious ___

back, to His fold ___ of ___ born a-gain ones. ___ Je - sus leads me in
foes. He ___ feeds me on a ta - ble spread, ___ My ___ cup of ___ bles - sings
place, with Je - sus ___ on ___ the - throne. ___ I am not a ___ stran - ger,

right - eous tracks as an a - dopt - ed daugh - ter or ___ son. ___
o - ver - flows. He pours the oil of bles - sing on my head. ___
nor a ___ guest, ___ but a child ___ safe ___ at ___ home. ___

Psalm 91
(Amplified by Attorney Joe Ragland)

I dwell in the secret (few know it) place of the most High.
I abide (rest) in the shade (staying under the cooling protection and safety)
    of the Almighty God.
I say of the Lord Jesus,
    You are my place of safety (refuge) and my protection (fortress),
    my God, in You I trust.

You deliver (rescue) me from the snare of the fowler (treacherous lure; hidden traps),
    and from deadly diseases (threats of sudden death).
You cover me with Your feathers (angels), and under Your wings I trust.
Your truth is my shield and buckler (armor to defend me).
I am not afraid of the terror (hunts to do me evil) by night;
    nor for the arrow (any weapon, evil plots, or slanders of the wicked formed against me)
    that flies by day; nor for the pestilence (epidemic; plague) that walks in darkness;
    nor for the destruction (calamity that spreads havoc) that destroys at noonday.
A thousand shall fall (die) at my side, and ten thousand at my
    right hand, but it shall not hurt (come near) me.
I will only watch (from a distance) and see the wicked punished (recompensed).

Because I have made the Lord Jesus, my habitation, no evil befalls (happens to) me,
    nor does any disaster (plague; blow) come to (even approach) my dwelling.
For the Lord Jesus gives His angels charge over me to keep me in all my ways.
They bear (catch; lift) me up in their hands, lest I dash my foot against a stone.
I tread on (they are under my feet) lions and serpents (all evil powers) and
    trample into the ground the young (having an angry prideful roar) lion and
    the dragon (the devil seeking to kill, steal, and destroy).

Because I have set my love on the Lord Jesus, He
    saves (protects, rescues) and honors me.
Jesus has set me on high because I have known His Name.
I call upon Jesus, and He answers me!

The Lord Jesus is with me in trouble (any distress).
He loves and delivers (rescues; honors) me!
With long life, He (Jesus) satisfies me and shows me
    His (today and throughout eternity) salvation!

Hallelujah

J. Ragland

L. Cohen

Now I've heard there was a Hea-ven a-bove. A se - cret place of safe-ty and love. But

ma - ny don't care, are a-shamed of Je - sus Christ, are you? The

bea-ten and cru - ci-fied, King of Glo - ry bids me come, the best thing I've e-ver done! Hal-le -

lu - jah! Hal-le - lu - jah! Hal-le - lu - jah! Hal-le - lu - jah! Hal-le - lu -

jah! So I came in child-like faith, and was sur-prised by joy - ful-ly be - ing born a -

gain. In - stead of Hell, I a - woke in the age of grace on my way to

glo - rious Heav'n! Hal - le - lu - jah! Hal-le - lu - jah! Hal - le - lu - jah! Hal-le -

lu - jah! Hal-le - lu - jah! The Lo - ver of your soul in-vites you to the

wed - ding sup - per of the Lamb. I have my in-vite, and I can save you a seat as the wed-ding hall will be quite full! Hal – le – lu – jah! Hal – le – lu – jah! Hal – le –

lu – jah! Hal – le – lu – jah! Hal – le – lu – jah!

un – der-stand there is room for more, who – so – e – ver will may come. But

ma – ny don't care a – bout ma – ri – tal ro – mance, what a-bout you? Hal – le – lu –

jah! Hal – le – lu – jah! Hal – le – lu – jah! Hal – le – lu – jah!

Do you have faith and a de – sire to re–ceive such a great sal – va – tion?

joy-ful-ly sing the King of Glo – ry's Hal – le–lu – jah wed–ding song what a–bout you? Hal – le –

lu – jah! Hal–le – lu – jah! Hal – le – lu – jah! Hal – le – lu – jah! Hal – le – lu –

jah!

MINE EYES HAVE SEEN THE GLORY

Lyrics by Joe M. Ragland

Battle Hymn of the Republic (19th C.)

1. Mine eyes have seen the glo - ry of the sal - va - tion of the Lord! He is
2. Man - y souls a - shamed of Je - sus will say, 'Moun - tains fall on us, and
3. I am not a - shamed of the Lamb of God who died for all my sins. What a - bout
4. Oh, be swift to re - pen - tance and re - ceive e - ter - nal life! As He

sift - ing chaff out from the wheat be - fore His judg - ment seat. Re -
hide us from the wrath of the One en - throned and from the Lamb!' Bro - thers,
you? Don't ne - glect such an of - fer of sal - va - tion great! He will
died to make men ho - ly, let us live to make men free. Yes! our

pent and so be saved or face His ter - ri - ble swift sword. His sal -
sis - ters come to - day, the Earth is ripe for har - vest time, there is
sound the fi - nal trum - pet, and the dead will rise up first, and those a -
Sa - vior's yoke is eas - y and His bur - den is light. Come just

va - tion is march - ing on! Glo - ry, glo - ry, hal - le - lu - jah! Glo - ry, glo - ry, hal - le -
al - ways room for more!
live will be with God for - ev - er!
as you are, for He will not re - ject you.

lu - jah! Glo - ry, glo - ry, hal - le - lu - jah! His sal - va - tion is march - ing on.

AFTERWORD POEM
FOR THE ADVENTURER

Youth and Romance

By

Joe M. Ragland, J.D., LL.M., LL.D., Esquire

Youth and romance are not a time of life,
but a state of mind,
not just finding a husband or a wife,
but a matter of the will,
a quality of a beautiful soul,
a time of brightness and vigor of the
emotions, and of the bounce and freshness
of the deep springs within.

Youth and romance mean courage over
timidity of the appetite,
exploring and adventures over
the love of ease.

Nobody grows old and feeble merely by a number of years,
but with a "poor me" pessimism of regrets,
looking back, choosing not
to forget things forgiven,
judging the faults of others,
and of deserting one's dreams and ideals.

I reach forth in the joyful now and to the good things daily
coming my way as I love God and rejoice in Him.

Years may wrinkle the skin, but to give up
the enthusiasm of life wrinkles the soul.
Let me smiling declare, "That's your problem,
angry and unhappy individual, reckless driver,
prejudice-bitter person, not mine! I refuse to
let you infect me with your negative vibes
as I hardly even notice a suffered wrong."

In my heart is the love of the wonder of it all,
having the unfailing childlike appetite of enjoying
today and laughing at the days to come.

In my heart is a wireless station of receiving
and giving messages of love, cheer, courage, beauty,
and the power of the Holy Spirit living in me.

I catch the little foxes of life, having all junk mail securely blocked.

I receive and give out waves of optimism,
being satisfied with my lot in life,
even into my eighties and nineties and then
throughout eternity with the joy of
my Lord and Savior giving me strength, youth,
and, yes, romance, and all these abundantly.

Ever since time began, nothing has ever
been found stronger than love!

When my Lord has tried me under
"The Law of Love,"
I shall come forth as gold
to a place where I'll be safe!

Sincerely Agape Yours,

Joe M. Ragland

Soli Deo Gloria†

www.ingramcontent.com/pod-product-compliance
Lightning Source LLC
LaVergne TN
LVHW061218060426
835508LV00014B/1344